Our Stupid
Relationships

Corey G. Carolina

Printed in the United States of America

First Printing, 2020

ISBN 978-0-9975092-2-9

Rise and Develop Publishing

Visit- www.CoreyCarolina.com

Email-corey@coreycarolina.com

Our Stupid Relationships

Corey G. Carolina

Table of Contents

INTRODUCTION

I want to thank all of you for being interested enough to purchase this book from an unknown author. My name is Corey Carolina – yes, just like the states. I have been gaining experience to write this book for most of my life.

As you all may know, relationships are extremely difficult. Some people can identify with having done things in the name of love, but when we look back at a previous relationship, we say, "Wow, I was stupid." That is the premise for this book. I have often reflected on past situations and realized how stupid I was to either do or say a particular thing, and you have, too.

I do not claim to be an expert on relationships, and this book is not an end-all, be-all for understanding interpersonal human reactions, but it may compel you to look at your past or current thinking and question it. I hope to help people understand how senseless we can be sometimes. So, sit back and enjoy this book, and please keep an open mind about what you are going to read. Look realistically and honestly at your own situation to see if you are being stupid – acting in a reckless manner that could harm yourself or others, as I know I have done in the past.

I do not want my readers to think I am attacking them or being judgmental. I simply want to share information I have gathered throughout my lifetime and discussions I have had with other people. We can all use help with our relationships, and this book provides a few pointers to how we can improve those relationships and try to keep ourselves from looking or feeling foolish. This book will help you analyze your relationships and evaluate what avenues are best for you to pursue. Not all interpersonal associations are the traditional boyfriend-girlfriend relationships. But when you stop and think about it, the boyfriend-girlfriend stereotype wasn't really a traditional relationship, anyway. I have been involved in many relationships; some were romantically inclined, while others would be defined more as close friendship – what some might describe as "kicking it."

"Kicking it" can describe a variety of situations, depending on the two people who are "kicking it." To some, it means just having sex with no commitment to exclusivity. Others may be getting to know each other without assuming the titles of "boyfriend" and "girlfriend." Think about it: What is your definition?

I hope this book will spark discussions on how readers can improve their relationships. This book focuses on romantic relationships, but the same techniques that can be used in these situations can also help improve other personal or professional relationships. If we strengthen our relationships, we should be able to understand one another better. Significant and healthy

Our Stupid Relationships

relationships are vital to our personal success and happiness, so it is important to nurture relationships.

Unfortunately, we all have to end or alter relationships, depending on current situations. How many friends or family members have you had to distance yourself from because they were just not right for you at the moment? How many romantic relationships have you had to end because they were toxic or unhealthy? Finally, how many relationships have you been blessed to still maintain after 10, 15, or 20 years?

Since the day of our first crush, we have all had feelings for someone and we may not have known whether that person reciprocated our emotions. I recall my first real crush, on a beautiful young girl in elementary school. She was so sweet, and had captivating eyes, luxuriant long hair, and beautiful straight teeth. In my young mind, she was the complete package. I saw myself as a hopeless romantic. I remember buying her a plush heart and candy for Valentine's Day, and I mustered the courage to give it to her the next day. I think she really appreciated it, because she smiled and thanked me. I was at the top of the world. To me, it was as if we had sealed our commitment with marriage, and I thought we would be together for the rest of our lives. This is the type of effect women can have on men, at whatever age – and no doubt the reverse is true, too.

As I look back now, I realize we were too young to understand or embrace with the concept of "boyfriend and girlfriend." In fact, I was in the dreaded "friend zone"; she didn't see me the same way I saw her. That was the first moment of my life in which I felt stupid in a relationship. If I had it to do all over again, would I? You'd better believe it. Sometimes it's worth it to put yourself out there and make yourself vulnerable to being stupid. As I aged, I understood more about the "friend zone" and how I never wanted to be in that place again.

Another relationship I remember from my youth was one millions of people have to endure: the relationship with myself. As adults, most of us understand we cannot be in successful relationships if we are not comfortable with ourselves. Are you depressed? Do you have baggage you are clinging to, mentally and physically? Do you love yourself? Do you trust others? Have you been abused? Are you confused about your sexuality? Are you curious about dating someone from another race? Have you gained weight? Do you have stretch marks? Did you go through a difficult disease from which you are recovering? Did you lose a family member? Were you fired from a job? Did he or she cheat on you? The list can go on and on. We have to love ourselves before we can truly love another person.

Whatever situation you are in, you have the power to make it better. It may take a few years, but you can do it by taking the first step and identifying what is wrong with the relationship. Unfortunately, sometimes you are the problem.

I believe that as a youth, I was well liked. I was not a bully or intentionally mean to others, but I do feel I was gullible. I decided in middle school to stop being so naive. That does not mean I stopped being gullible at that time, but at least I had that conversation with myself and was determined to work on it.

That internal dialogue happened after I once again felt stupid in a relationship. I fell for another beautiful girl, who was new to my middle school and rode my bus. I saw her for the first time and fell in love – at least, "puppy love" – with her. To me, she was one of the prettiest girls in school. I was shy and probably wouldn't have asked her for her number, but she beat me to the punch. Her sister told me one day on the bus that her sister liked me. I tried to pretend it wasn't a big deal, but I was jumping for joy inside. This young girl was far more physically developed than most of the seventh- or eight-grade girls and more experienced in relationships than I was. Not only had she tasted her first kiss, but also she had already had sexual intercourse. I was way out of my league, but of course, I couldn't admit that.

My mother hated this girl because she felt she was too much for me. We dated for less than six months, but I really liked her. She would ask me if she could take my virginity, and I would just mumble something like, "I don't know." My first kiss was with her. She came over to my house one night on her way to the club – and she was still in the seventh grade! Before she left to get in the car with friends, we kissed. It had to be her worst kiss ever. My teeth were clanking against hers. It was embarrassing, but she did not make me feel clumsy or insecure.

Not long after that, we broke up. Come to find out, my mom called her and told her she had to break up with me. A couple weeks after that, I saw her cuddling with another guy who was on our football team. He was more experienced than I in the sex department, and had a reputation as being a bit of a bad boy, so I think that was more to her liking. I felt so stupid after I thought about how quickly she moved on to someone else whom I knew, and it occurred to me that she might have been seeing other young men when she was going to the club. I really should have listened to my mother, but in hindsight, I suspect I got lucky that we broke up. I may have made a bad decision and had sex with her, and I could have had a child too early in life.

My next two relationships had similar endings. The first started when I was a sophomore in high school. I met a young lady at the Tulsa Indoor Fun Fair who was a freshman in high school. I loved her little nerdy glasses, and she had the cutest smile. When I first saw her, she was with a guy I knew from middle school. I was with some of my friends, so I felt emboldened. I asked the guy if she was his girlfriend. He said yes, but I remember her glancing up at him that suggested, "No, he isn't; he just lied." I took that expression as an invitation to get to know more about her.

My friends and I talked to them for a few more minutes, and then we walked off. I thought about her for the rest of the night. I felt I had to find out more about her. I did not really like the guy who she was with, so I did not have any loyalty to

Our Stupid Relationships

him. We did have a friend in common, so I called her to inquire about the girl with the funny glasses. She confirmed the girl was not actually that guy's steady. My friend told me she just didn't want to hurt his feelings or make him look bad in front of my friends and me. I became even more intrigued, and asked our mutual friend to share her phone number. My friend let me know that this girl's mother was very strict and that she wasn't allowed to date or get out of the house much. I didn't care; I had to speak with her.

We finally talked on the phone, and we had an instant connection. We started talking more and more and eventually began dating. It was a bit annoying, because I could not see her regularly. For one thing, I worked long hours, so I didn't have a lot of free time. I eventually got frustrated with not being able to see her. I remember a conversation during which I told her I was getting tired of us planning opportunities to see each other, but she would usually cancel.

I told her that the next time she called off a date, I was going to call it quits with her. Not more than a week passed before she cancelled on me again. She spoke with me that night and asked if I was going to do what I said I would. I took that as a challenge, so I said yes. We broke up that night, though we stayed in contact and talked off and on through high school. We eventually met back up when we attended the same college.

The sparks ignited again. I fell in love with her, but I was new to that university and I did not want to be tied down to one woman. That did not sit well with her. Another guy was very interested in her, and she started hanging out with him. Now I couldn't tolerate that! I truly loved her and wanted to be with her, but at the same time, I was foolish. I decided I wanted to be with her and I would fight to make sure she chose me over the other guy.

I wrote her a four-page letter and convinced her residential adviser to let me into her room so I could leave it on her bed. Once she read the letter, she called me and confessed her love for me, and we started dating again. We were a perfect couple. We had fun with each other, we enjoyed our conversations, and we loved the idea that we both wanted to be successful. Our relationship went on for a couple years without any major hitches.

The relationship took a turn for the worse when she started going back home on the weekends to go to church. Now I am all for someone getting closer to the lord, but when she returned to campus on Sunday evenings, she was different. She started to pull away from me. Her excuse was that some women at her church, who had never met me, felt I was an impediment to her spiritual journey. She also said the women considered me a distraction from her from her college workload. I was so upset because at the time, I was in a meeting each day of the week and studying multiple hours per day, so I did not get to see her except in the evening. She was also busy with organizations and studying. I told her I didn't appreciate her taking the advice of these women who did not know me. This was the same excuse my next girlfriend gave.

I still felt it was not fair that she was making a decision without allowing me to have any input. I was hurt, and I let my hurt turn into anger. I felt she had crushed me and everyone would know. I thought at the time that we would eventually get married, or at least be in a long-term relationship, but she allowed others to convince her I was a problem. She ended our relationship, and I made the decision at that moment that if she ever tried to get back together with me, I would turn her down. I felt so stupid because I gave my heart to her, and she threw away our relationship.

"I am a lover and you crushed my heart. I gave my whole being to you, and you broke my heart." How many times have you had these thoughts? I remember being heartbroken from that relationship, feeling vulnerable and lost. I thought I was trying to be a good boyfriend, but my girlfriend decided I wasn't good enough for her any longer. I adored this young woman because she was perfect for me. She was so cute with her little glasses and she was funny. We instantly connected because we were both fun-loving people. She was ambitious and goal-oriented, just like I was. The only thing that held me back was her family.

It is important for me to have a good relationship with a mate's family, and I did not have a good history with hers. Her mother once accused me of persuading her to skip school. That caused a problem with my own mother, who called me and scolded me for helping my ex cut class. She said she had spoken with my ex's mother and wanted answers about my involvement. I told my mother I had nothing to do with that. I explained to my mother that I did not even have a car, so how was I going to drive to her school to get her out of class? My ex-girlfriend's stepfather even called me, and he scared the hell out of me. He told me he knew I helped her skip and he was a law officer, so I'd better tell him the truth. I happened to be out of school because we had a scheduled day off for parent-teacher conferences. Now I may or may not have seen her that day, but I did not go get her out of school.

The final relationship that made me feel stupid started in high school as well. This young woman was different from those in any previous relationship I had because she was in a grade above me. I was a sophomore in high school and she was a junior. We met through a mutual friend whom I worked with. I trusted that friend because we had become close while I was working at our local amusement park. She knew my previous relationships had not worked out, and she told me she had a very sweet friend she wanted me to meet. I was skeptical because I had never been on a blind date. But I was intrigued after I learned she was on the dance team, very smart, and well liked at school. She also attended church regularly.

My friend told me she would ask this girl to drop by our job site to meet me. I was nervous and I wondered if she would be interested in me. She went to a different school, and she was used to a different kind of guy; she had previously dated an older guy who was more experienced in relationships than I was. I agreed to at least meet her to see if I liked her. She had her friend come to the amusement park one night while I was working. I took my lunch when she got there so we could walk around the park and talk. She seemed very nice and had a great smile. I said to myself, "Dang, I hope she is interested in me."

I was extremely nervous while we were walking around, hoping I was not talking too much or acting too nerdy. I did not want to come off as too macho, nor did I want to seem too timid. At the end of my lunch, I felt I could have walked and talked with her for days. We instantly connected. My friend had really come through for me. She knew I wanted a good young lady and she helped me find one.

My new friend and I started to talk on the phone almost every night. We discussed our first date with our mutual friend and her boyfriend. We decided to go to the haunted house in town. When we first showed up to the haunted house, we were a bit uncomfortable, but when we started to walk through the exhibit, we began holding hands and holding each other. By the end of the night, we were "in like" with each other.

As the months passed, I was able to meet her family. Her father is a great man, and he welcomed me with open arms, which I respected. He and I eventually built a strong relationship, and I looked upon him as a father figure. Her sisters and brothers were some of the nicest people I had been around. I started attending her church and everyone was so welcoming. I am still a member of that church, almost 18 years later. We decided to get into a relationship, but with boundaries. We were both virgins, and she wanted us to stay that way until we got married. I didn't have a problem with that, because at that time, I was not interested in having sex. I was more interested in school and football.

Our relationship continued to grow over the next two years, and it was a good one. We went to each other's proms, and most people thought we were a nearly perfect couple. As I went into my junior year in high school and she went into her senior year, we had a difficult decision to make. We had to decide what we would do when she went off to college. I wanted to continue a relationship with her, but I knew there would be older and more experienced guys in college and I would have to compete for her love.

Once it came time for her to leave, we promised each other we would try to keep our relationship going. But after a few months, while she was in Kansas, I felt her start to distance herself from me. I would call her, but she would not call me back for a couple days. The insecurity and jealously started to take hold when I thought about what she was doing that would prevent her from calling me back right away.

One night, I called her and had to leave another message. She called me back later that night, but I could tell something was different in her tone of voice. I let her know I had some uneasy feelings and I wanted to keep an open communication with her about that. I explained that I did not understand why we were not talking more than we were. She explained that she was busy with school and church. I let her know I understood because I worked at night, played football, and had class work to complete. The conversation took an interesting turn when I asked her if she still wanted to be in a relationship with me. She paused when I asked her that question.

I could tell something was wrong. She explained she was too busy for a long-distance relationship. My heart sank, and I asked her why she felt that way. She said I was keeping her from focusing on school and church. In my head, I was thinking, "How could I hold her back when she barely calls or sees me?" I was upset with the conversation because I had tried hard to keep our relationship together, and she was now throwing it all away. I told her I had to call her back because I was confused and angry, but I wanted to make sure I stayed respectful. Who could have known I would have the same type of conversation a few years later with a previous girlfriend?

I called my friend Tyrone, who was the boyfriend of my friend who introduced me to my girlfriend. He was older than me and had more experience with relationships. I explained the entire phone conversation to him. He told me that story did not add up and that something else was wrong. He advised me to call her back and push her for the real reason she wanted to call it quits. He said he had a similar issue with his girlfriend, so he suspected there might be something else she was not sharing.

I called my girlfriend back and I pressed her for more details. I let her know I did not believe her excuse for wanting to break up was the truth. I told her I did not see how I could be keeping her from focusing on school or church, since I was not able to communicate with her frequently. I was so angry with her, and I kept pressing her to tell me the real reason she wanted to break up.

She eventually admitted she had met someone while attending college. My world fell apart when she said that. She told me she had been riding with her cousin to visit her cousin's boyfriend, and she was introduced to his friend. According to her, they started hanging out and had just kissed. I told her I did not believe that's all they had done.

I was blindsided and I felt stupid for trying so hard to keep our relationship together, while she was making out with someone else. Other young women wanted to be in a relationship with me at that time, but I did not give those opportunities a chance because I was loyal, and I wanted to make the long-distance relationship with my girlfriend work. The woman I thought I could have married had crushed my heart. We maintained a distant friendship after the breakup for a few years and even tried to rekindle it a couple of times, but it wasn't the same. She made me feel stupid for falling in love with her.

CHAPTER ONE

What does it mean to be STUPID?

The word "stupid" can be very harsh in some contexts, but when it comes to relationships, it is not meant to be derogatory, but rather to be an expressive term to get people to think. No one wants to be viewed as stupid, but we still allow others to take advantage of us and keep ourselves in certain negative situations for a variety of reasons.

Think about the last time you gave advice to one of your friends about what he or she should do in a relationship. You may have felt the friend was being stupid in that situation, but you gave him the best advice you could. You do not think he is a stupid person at his core, but maybe just in that particular situation. That is what being stupid means in this book. I have been in multiple relationships that have made me feel stupid, and I wished afterward that I could have seen the warning signs.

If you can think about your relationships in an objective way, you will perceive where you are being stupid, and in doing so, you can find solutions to your problems. It is hard to stand outside of a relationship and dispassionately evaluate your options. We find ourselves in love and unable to see beyond our day-to-day involvement with the person. We allow things to happen in our relationships that we would view as crazy if we saw someone else in the same situation. The key is to stop and evaluate your relationships and decide what your best options should be.

The state of stupidity is not fun; it's embarrassing and demeaning. People do not set out to look stupid to others; they aim to look as good as they can. But relationships are full of stupidies, and there are a number of clues someone is making you look stupid in your relationship.

How do you prevent yourself from looking stupid in a relationship? Think about your past relationships and recall any time you felt you should have done something differently or made an alternate decision. You may have even recognized a red flag that you simply ignored.

With the advancement of technology, texting and messaging have become dominant forms of communication. I have my phone with me most of the day, reading and sending messages. This technology has also created its own stupid situations. Many discover their significant others have been cheating after finding incriminating messages on their phones or on social media platforms. People have a right to be concerned if their significant others are constantly on their phones and not spending quality time with them. Some people would rather end their relationships instead of giving up their phone or social media passwords. That does not immediately signal guilt, but it does indicate you should be concerned.

I am not an advocate for snooping, but an open dialogue is important. If you are comfortable with the significant other's hiding the phone when texts come in, that's your business. But if you suspect you may find yourself looking stupid one day because you did not ask basic questions, you may want to have a conversation with your significant other.

Social media can and will affect any relationship. The main sites people now frequent are Facebook, Twitter, Instagram, LinkedIn, and a few others. These platforms allow people to socialize with one another just by posting comments or "liking" photos. There are also opportunities to become immersed in situations that are dangerous for relationships. A person may be looking through photos from friends, when suddenly a message comes through from and ex-boyfriend or ex-girlfriend. The contact may start off harmless, but then turn to reminiscing about the past. A meeting for lunch could happen, and it could go further from there, all without the significant other's knowing what's going on.

It's tough trying to maintain loyalty in a relationship when you do not know for sure if your significant other is doing the same. Some people would say if you do not feel you can trust someone, you do not need to be involved with that individual. But it's not that easy in every case. You may have children with your significant other, or you may have built a life together. Even so, no relationship is worth being stupid for. If you see warning signs, such as incriminating social media posts or text messages, it is worth a conversation to ensure you are making the best decision on how to move forward or protect yourself from being snared in a stupid situation.

I have made people feel stupid before, and it is a horrible feeling. I have lied to get things I wanted and have led others to think they were the only women I was seeing at the time. I know how it is to feel stupid and to make someone else feel stupid as well. It is important to always consider how you will affect someone else by your actions. If you decide to cheat on your mate, it can impact that person for years to come. There may also be negative ramifications in your ex-mate's future relationships.

Yes, I have had my heart broken a few times. That is not a pain I want others to endure, but I know it's going to happen. People will marry cheating spouses, and they will allow themselves to stay in abusive relationships. My goal is to reach as many people as possible to help them stay out of stupid relationships or situations.

CHAPTER TWO

I Do Not Want to Be Pretty; I Want to Be Loved

It is a mistake to think all the pretty women in the world have it easy when it comes to relationships. Some may assume they would not have a hard time finding others to love them. But that is incorrect. Attractive women deal with some of the same issues everyone else deals with. One only has to look at some of the actors, business leaders, athletes, and single mothers to understand that.

Relationships involve dealing with other humans, and humans make mistakes: They cheat, they abuse, and they take advantage of others. There have been a number of people who may be considered pretty who have had a hard time finding Mr. or Ms. Right.

When I was having a discussion with a young woman, she told me she was tired of being called "pretty" by other men. She was tired of hearing all the good things about her outward appearance. She wanted a man who was interested in knowing more about her mind and heart, instead of her face and feminine features. This is very important to understand, because at times, men suspect women just want to hear how pretty they are or how good they look in certain outfits. It's true that women do want to hear those things, but they also want to know men have a genuine interest in them intellectually, spiritually, and emotionally. The lady of whom I am speaking is definitely beautiful, sexy, and smart, but that did not define her.

I believe women who allow themselves to be manipulated by other men simply because they are handsome is not an effective use of their valuable time. Women or men would be better off using their time focusing on being the best people they can be in all facets of their lives. Any person can say another individual is cute, but the person you should hope for will look at you without makeup, with bad breath, with crust in your eyes, having a bad hair day, and still love being in your presence.

True love can be hard to find, but if a person can love you for whom you really are, then you are one of the fortunate ones. Men are not too complex; they want women who can not only stimulate them visually or sexually, but who can challenge them, believe in their dreams, show interest in their interests, and respect their mothers. Now thousands of women can say, "I did all of that and my man still left me or cheated." But love is not an exact science, and unfortunately, some of us end up being stuck in stupid relationships with stupid people.

Why would a man leave a woman who loves him, has sex with him on a regular basis, shows interest in his interests, loves his mother, and tries to provide for the household the same as he does? The answer: He is stupid. Both men and women make stupid mistakes. Men and women cheat, lie, manipulate, hurt, and make others feel stupid. The goal should be to recognize warning signs, which are meant to spark a conversation or review of your relationships to hopefully keep you from being in a stupid situation.

People want to find mates to whom they are attracted, and unfortunately, the first impression of someone is usually based on how he or she looks. But looks aren't everything, and they eventually fade — which everyone understands on some level. Think about older couples you have seen, exhibiting the same amount of love as if they were new to their relationships. How do they do it? They love their mates for who they are and what they bring to the relationship. That is the key. How do you find someone you can love even when you are 65 years old?

A person's appearance is only the mask that covers the internal self. What you have to figure out is what kind of internal person you are looking for in a mate. You may go through a few relationships and after they are done, you realize you made some stupid mistakes. Life is about making mistakes and learning from them. Life is also about learning from other people's mistakes and trying not to make the same ones yourself.

Upon further conversation with the aforementioned young lady, I realized she was like so many people I knew. She was very cute with beautiful eyes and a great body. She had a flirty laugh and pretty teeth. She had a few sexy tattoos and a smile that would melt a man's heart. She would be a good mate for a lot of men. She told me when she goes out, she wants to look good — not to catch a mate, but because she likes to keep herself looking nice.

Corey G. Carolina

She said when a man approaches her, the first thing he says is that she is beautiful. But she already knows she is very nice-looking and she does not need the validation from a stranger. She would prefer they introduce themselves and speak to her on an intellectual level. She wants to see where their heads are and what type of people they are. She was recently divorced and has two children, and she really loved her ex-husband. She felt she was a failure for not keeping her marriage together. I did not get into the specifics of why they divorced, but I suspect he turned out not to be the man she thought she had married. She felt stupid for not seeing the warning signs.

You can be the prettiest woman in the world and still find yourself feeling stupid in relationships. How many popular girls in high school actually married the boys they felt they were so in love with? How many boys thought that although their girlfriends went off to college and they were still seniors in high school, the girls would be faithful but then, that wasn't the case? Relationships are full of stupid moments, but those moments do not have to define who you are.

You have to be a detective when you are meeting potential mates or friends. If you can identify traits that are deal-breakers in the first few conversations, you can protect yourself from a heartache years down the road. People are not going to be themselves during initial meetings, so you have to find a way to get the information you want in the way you ask questions.

It is OK to ask tough questions in the beginning of a relationship, because you have to limit your exposure to negative people who will ruin not only that relationship, but may even damage others you have. In this day of social media, you can find out a great deal about someone by just looking through his or her posts and photos. We all "stalk" on social media from time to time, and it is OK to look through social media to learn more about other people. It is even smart to look for them on YouTube to see if they have any videos out there of themselves talking. This may give you more insight to who they are. This is not a foolproof plan, because you may discover old things about someone who has changed or matured since posting earlier comments, pictures, and videos.

Another scenario is a young lady who was, once again, very attractive, smart, and driven. She was younger than the previous woman, but her story is just as interesting. She was a "relationship junkie," so she felt she needed to have a boyfriend at all times. You may be, or may know someone, who feels the same way. Her thought was that she enjoyed relationships, so why not be in one if she found someone she liked? It makes sense, in a way, but I believe it is a dangerous mentality to have. What that does is open you up for short-term relationships that do not yield very much of a benefit.

Everyone recognizes there is a double standard about men who date a number of women, versus women who date a number of men. That may not be fair, but since it remains a societal norm, women have to be a bit pickier about whom they date. In reality, men should do the same. Do you find yourself in a six-month relationship every six months? Do you find yourself sleeping with someone with the thought that you all may get into a serious relationship at some point? Do you think you need to hop into a relationship three months after you meet someone? If any of these questions describe you or someone you know, it sets up you or your friend for a series of stupid relationships.

You may find out things about someone whom you've slept with or moved into your house that you never thought to ask about early in the relationship. Though it remains a misconception in the mind of many vulnerable people, sleeping with someone will not make that person want to be in a relationship. I am not necessarily saying you have to wait until marriage to have sex, unless that is something you feel strongly about. I believe that adults should be able to make decisions about whom they want for mates, and if the feeling is right, they should make a move to start a relationship with reserved optimism. Relationships are great, but red flags are everywhere, and you must be able to see them.

It's important to understand that if you jump into relationships without asking difficult questions for which you need answers, the outcome may or may not be what you hope for. If your past two or three relationships started with sex within a few weeks or months and you find out you are not getting the results you want, you may want to wait for sex just a bit longer the next time around. If the man or woman gets frustrated and stops talking to you, you've just saved yourself a potential lifetime of heartaches and problems.

If you are not interested in an exclusive relationship and you prefer to date several men or women, that's up to you. But you may want to let your dates know up-front that you are not interested in a relationship right now, so they get a better

Our Stupid Relationships

understanding of what to expect. Women should be able to play the field just like men to find love, if that's what they want.

At one time, I was convinced that there were thousands of women who were willing to "settle" in a relationship. When I am out in public, I see so many pretty women who are with guys whom I think are a step down. That may seem shallow on my part, but I know my friends and I have all said at one time or another, "How did he get HER?" You can see the same thing with men, where observers may think a guy is far more attractive than his mate, but this situation seems more common with women. There's nothing wrong with that, because I feel my wife is far cuter than I am and that she could have found a more handsome guy if she wanted.

As I have grown older, I have come to suspect that these women aren't just "settling" at all. Women, I believe, are not merely visual people; they fall for the person, the personality, the potential, the ability to make them laugh or feel comforted, a faith in God, and more. Some men, including myself, look at the outward appearance first, but then grow to be more interested in the personality of the woman than just her looks. There are few things more disconcerting than a fine-looking woman with a horrible personality.

CHAPTER THREE

How do I know if I am being STUPID?

I define "stupid," for the purposes of this book, to mean doing things, saying things, and acting in a certain fashion. Being stupid in a relationship is something a number of people, including myself, have experienced either during a relationship or after the relationship has ended. It is funny how you do not see some things while you are in a relationship. It is hard to fly above the relationship and look down on what is really going on.

Being stupid in a relationship does not mean you are a stupid person, nor does it mean your partner is stupid. It just means you have allowed love to blind you at times, when deep inside, you know what you should do or say. For example, think about the last time you have questioned an aspect of your relationship but have overlooked it only to find out later, after the relationship had ended, that you should have followed your gut. Your mind will usually tell you things your heart will not. Your heart may provide life to your body and the ability to love others, but your mind makes the decisions on what is right and what is wrong. The problem is, we tend to live our lives with our hearts instead of our minds. Generally, the mind knows the best action to take and can identify the true reality of a certain situation.

Do you ever have the feeling something is just not right in a relationship? Do you think, "There is more to the story than my mate is leading me to believe"? In a number of situations, you should listen to your questions and push for clear answers. You are a special person and you deserve everything you want in a relationship. You don't deserve to feel you have been taken advantage of or that you have been made to look stupid in a given situation. Your questions may be the result of your mind and heart trying to work together to make sense of your relationship. Your heart wants to believe your mate is good and honest, but your mind wants to ensure that your mate is meeting your requirements.

It is sometimes difficult to make decisions that are the best for you. You may know your relationship is not healthy, but you may stay in it for a number of reasons of which you constantly remind yourself. Those reasons could be that you feel you love your mate; you do not want to be alone; you do not think you can find anyone else like your mate; you do not want to start a new relationship; and the list can go on for pages. You have to stop thinking the situation is going to magically work itself out. If your mate is immature and you do not see a change in the near future, you need to ask yourself if you are willing to wait for this person to grow up, or if you are going to focus on yourself and your personal growth. Though it is difficult for people to think about themselves in their relationships, you owe it to yourself to focus on what is best for you, and make decisions accordingly.

Do not be afraid to make decisions that may end your relationship. If the relationship is worth saving, you and your mate will work it out. Some of the best decisions you can make while in your relationship may require you to think twice, but that's OK, because you want to make a decision you can live with. Life is full of decisions you must make, and the correct decision in a relationship can save your life. Just think about the people who felt they should get out of the relationship but did not, and they are no longer with us. Crazy things happen, and you have to keep yourself in the forefront.

If you are in a relationship and you have not met your mate's close friends or family, you need to find out why that has not happened. A person who values you as a partner will be eager to introduce you to the most important people in his or her life. I am not saying you need to meet the parents in the first couple days or weeks, but if you have been with someone for six months and you have not hung out with your partner's friends on a regular basis, that signals a problem.

Remember you want to limit your "stupid" opportunities; you do not want to let anyone make you look stupid. I have seen relationships where the woman was with her partner for four or five years but really did not know that partner's family, and the partner did not know her family. If your mate does not show interest in meeting your friends or family, you should run! A person who is interested in you will be interested in where you come from and what type of family and friends you have.

I hear about relationships that end after cheating occurs. We have all seen them on social media. One day, you see pictures of them at an event, seemingly happy. The next day, you see posts about their break-up. I always wonder what warning signs were present in the relationship that was missed at a crucial moment.

Being stupid in relationships seems to happen to everyone at some point. That's because people are people. Some people change their attitudes from day to day. Some use excuses of being stressed or depressed to justify their cheating. But there are better ways to deal with stress or depression than cheating on your mate. If you know your worth, you should know how to appreciate someone whom you feel is worthy of your love. And if you know your worth, you will not allow another person to make you feel stupid in your relationship. Sometimes, it takes a negative occurrence in a relationship to open our eyes to the reality.

Could you have prevented the negative things? Possibly, if you had looked for clues in your mate's behavior or actions. I am not telling anyone to be a private investigator, but you should instinctively know when something is wrong in your relationship. Find out why you feel that way. There is a reason your heart and mind are trying to protect your feelings and working to keep you from feeling stupid in relationships.

CHAPTER FOUR

Is Your Mate Cheating?

This is the question so many people ask themselves on a day-to-day basis. No one wants to look stupid and find out a mate has been unfaithful in the relationship. We sometimes feel stupid when we find out our mate has been cheating, because we know there were so many clues we ignored.

Think about a situation when you knew you should have questioned your mate but you decided not to do so, for your own reasons. Perhaps you didn't want to appear to be a nagging or an untrusting person. You may not have wanted to upset your mate or start an argument, or you may not really want to know the answers to your questions. It is so easy to ignore what we do not want to see.

If you have ever cheated on someone, you know how devastating it can be when your mate finds out. And if you have been cheated on, you also know how devastating it is to be betrayed. Cheating is an action that may be different for every person. Some people cheat because they feel it is the only alternative to happiness. Others may cheat for the thrill, to fulfill the urge to be loved or to feel sexy. Cheating is a sickness that may need some professional assistance to overcome. It is difficult to get into the mode of being a cheater and then to just stop cold turkey. It can be done, but first, such people must really want to evaluate themselves internally and see if the people they are cheating on deserve to be treated in such a way.

If your mate is not holding your attention, communicate that, and try to work through your issues. Give your mate the common courtesy to try to change to meet your needs. If you are an extremely sexual person and your mate is not, you may have a great deal of work to do to make the relationship succeed. You do not want to end up regretting the selection of your mate and then express that regret by cheating simply because that person is not sexual enough for you. You also want to be honest with yourself. If you cannot deal with your mate's lower sex drive, a straight conversation needs to take place to determine if a compromise can be reached.

If your mate will not conform or compromise, it is probably best to move on and find another more compatible relationship, or remain single for as long as you deem appropriate. That is easier said than done, but you do not want to get into the mode of looking for amazing sex from someone else, because you will ruin your relationship. If you have children together or have been in a long-term relationship, it's extremely difficult to make the decision to end the relationship, but ask yourself if it's better to cheat on your mate or just break up. If your choice is to stay in the relationship and find someone who can satisfy your sexual needs on the side, just remember those sexually satisfying moments can only last for a brief time before disaster occurs. You may convince yourself you can just have sex with no emotional commitment, but you never know how the arrangement is going to affect the person with whom you are cheating. The last thing you want is for your new sexual partner to become attached to you and want to be the main person in your life. This will make it difficult, if not impossible, to keep your primary relationship intact.

All of us want to know how to spot a potential cheater, but it is difficult to identify a person who has those tendencies. The best thing to do is to always be on the defensive. Keep your eyes open to all things that may concern you. If you think someone is not being truthful with you, just ask the question of your concern. It may be easy for your mate to lie to you, you have to be aware of that when communicating. Usually if a person is acting out of the ordinary, there may be a cause for concern. You do not have to get in your mate's face and level accusations of wrongdoing, but you should be able to talk to your mate and address your concerns. If you do not feel comfortable talking to your mate, you should re-evaluate your relationship. If you feel your mate will get angry, yell at you, hit you, throw things, punch things, storm out, or ignore you, think about ending the relationship unless the person is willing to aggressively work on changing to meet your criteria. These are not excuses for actions that may lead to your mate's cheating, but there are usually underlying reasons for why people cheat.

A lack of effective communication can be a factor in cheating. If you and your mate are not on the same page about your relationship, you may find yourself loving someone who merely likes you in return. You may be giving everything of yourself, while your mate is just taking everything and giving nothing back. You must effectively communicate your wants and needs with your mate. You also have to be clear about your goals with your relationship. If your mate knows exactly what you are thinking, there will be no cause for guessing and speculation.

It is stupid to think your mate will never do anything to hurt you or cheat on you. Your mate may love you with all of his or her heart, but that will not guarantee cheating will never occur. Remember, sex and love are not the same thing, though one can enhance the other, so you must protect yourself.

Another factor that will lead to cheating is curiosity. A person who feels he or she has had to "settle" for something less than the ideal mate may venture off to look for a person who will meet their needs. This does not always have to be a sexual issue; your mate may be looking for an emotional or intellectual connection that is not being made with you. If your connection with your mate has decreased, try to find ways to reconnect. You may look at taking a weekend trip together to get away from your normal routine. It does not have to be an expensive cruise; it may be a short road trip. You may not even have to talk during the entire trip. Try just holding and rubbing each other's hands.

Connection is key to relationships. You must connect mentally and sexually. A sexual connection is healthy. Research shows that sex will help you lose weight, relieve stress, feel loved, and help you sleep. Sex must not be forced, but it should be something both mates want. If a person feels the mate is only having sex as a form of appeasement that can anger or deflate the partner who wants sex. One women with whom I was in a romantic relationship told me she only wanted to have sex 50 percent of the time that we engaged in it. This is an example of losing sexual connection. A portion of that lost connection was due to some issues she had with her appearance, and some of the problem was that I not making love to her mind.

Making love to your partner's mind means telling her how beautiful she is, or how handsome he is. It means expressing how much your partner means to you. It means pulling your weight with household chores and expenses. If you make love to your mate's mind, the body will follow. Your partner will also give more of herself, or himself, to you. You may be able to act out your fantasies with a mate who previously was not interested in sharing those fantasies with you.

Being a giver is the most important element in your relationship. You must give your heart, your mind, and your soul. Don't allow yourself to miss clues of potential issues; give your mate the most you have to give. If you feel you are not comfortable giving your full self to your mate, remember that your mate will be able to sense that you are holding back. If you feel your mate is not giving his or her full self, you may naturally suspect your mate is cheating. So, it's reasonable to expect your mate would be suspecting the same thing when the shoe is on the other foot.

CHAPTER FIVE

Never Trust Your Mate 100 Percent

It is important to have trust in your relationship, but you always want to keep your eyes open for warning signs to avoid being too vulnerable. I have been cheated on by people whom I have loved and never thought they would do that to me. I have also been in two relationships at the same time, and neither of the girls knew about the other. Not all men or women cheat on their partners; I believe a majority of people who have committed to a relationship truly want to do things right. However, most people, at one time or another, do at least think about cheating, even if they never act on it. My research indicates that thoughts of cheating usually crop up when an individual fails to address the needs of the mate.

Even if a mate is not getting what he or she wants out of a relationship, it is important to communicate the concerns to the significant other. Trust is built but not guaranteed, so you should always gauge the "trust-o-meter" before you get into a serious relationship. If your mate has had a string of bad relationships, it will take more time to build trust. I feel that I can never trust a significant other 100 percent, because we are all human and we all make mistakes. But I do not allow my innate suspicions to prevent me from falling in love. Love is an emotion that can set you up for failure, but it can also make your life complete.

The ability to recognize red flags is critical, especially when starting a relationship with someone who may not be on the same relationship time line as you are. Cheaters will tell you exactly whom they are if you can allow yourself to listen and observe their actions. The grass is not greener on the other side, but sometimes it is softer and more relaxing. If your words or actions create anger, resentment, or boredom, you may find yourself single or the victim of a cheating mate. If a mate is determined to cheat, there is nothing you can do to stop that from happening. Cheaters are generally selfish and self-absorbed, and another person's best efforts won't change that.

I have told friends in the past that to be a cheater, you must be a selfish person, and in some cases, a narcissistic one. Cheating is a very selfish act. When you know, you love someone or care for that person dearly, but you still allow your lust or even your mind to be occupied by someone else, that is a mark of selfishness. Cheating can also be used to hurt your mate. I have cheated in the past, and I know I have hurt others as a result. Many of my friends have also been in situations they wish they could have avoided because they hurt their mates.

A cheater wants to have that cake and eat it, too. A cheater wants to get the love and affection from a significant other, while at the same time getting love and affection from someone else. There are so many scenarios that lead people to cheat. The person may want to experience something more exciting. Cheating can be exciting, as with any other situation that involves sampling the "forbidden fruit." But lack of intimacy or attention to the mate can also be an impetus for cheating. Most human beings need affection, touching, sweet words, and comfort, and if they do not believe these things are important to their mates, they can use these perceived deficits as an opportunity to cheat.

Trust is important, but I do not believe in blind trust. You and your mate must build trust with each other, and that can take time. I personally believe that for your own emotional safety, even if you do trust your mate, you should retain about 5 to 10 percent skepticism. There is no need to bash your mate every time a red flag pops up, but you should stay alert to the possibility that your mate may be cheating. The last thing an individual wants to hear is that every little thing he or she does will exacerbate the insecurity of a mate. Your mate would most likely prefer to have conversations about how you can build a better relationship. You should try to enjoy your mate and cherish the time you have on Earth with those you love.

Many observers may think my views are skewed because I have been the victim of cheating in the past. That may be true, but those experiences have also made me a better person in relationships. Those experiences have allowed me to see the red flags relationships present. I also have a better understanding of what I will and will not accept in a relationship. In an odd way, I am thankful to my previous girlfriends and other individuals for molding me into the man I am today. Of course, in typical male fashion – and I say this with a wink and a chuckle – I will take credit for all the things I do right, but I will blame my exes for all the things I do wrong!

It is OK to be skeptical of your mate, but try not to allow that feeling to hinder your relationship. Even though you may have some reservations about your mate, you should still try to make the relationship work, if that's what you want. If your mate shows you he or she is not trustworthy, you have to decide if the relationship is worth salvaging.

CHAPTER SIX

Why Do You Keep Finding Losers?

It's a question countless people have asked themselves: "Why is everyone else finding love, but I am not?" Life is full of experiences, and you will go through many relationships. Some experiences will be good, and some will be bad. You may label someone a "loser" just because he or she fails to do what you want or demand, but that may be an erroneous classification.

To determine why you feel you are repeatedly drawn to "losers," you must first find out why you have been selecting particular types of mates. It may not necessarily be your fault, but it can be illuminating to take an honest look at yourself to determine what signals you are sending. When you know your own worth, you will attract people who want to treat you like you are worth a million dollars. That is not always the case, but it's true more often than not.

Your self-esteem is key to the type of person who is attracted to you. Men and women are both attracted to confidence and self-assurance. If you're confident in yourself, some people will find that intimidating, but you really don't want to be around those folks, anyway. Your goal is to find a partner who challenges you and helps make you a better person – emotionally, professionally, spiritually, and physically. You have to be confident in yourself and understand you do not need a mate to make you feel whole or important. You are the most important person in your own life, and you have to be at your best before you are ready to be in a relationship.

There is no guarantee you will ever find a mate who is not a "loser" by certain standards. You can find someone who is highly educated and successful in a career, but that does not mean he or she will not be a loser in your relationship. Your mate is less likely to go astray when motivated by the fear that you will end the relationship if he or she cheats or fails to appreciate you sufficiently. Your mate should not be afraid you will do bodily harm, but should know you have standards, and if those are not met, the relationship is not the right one for you.

Potential mates need to understand that while you may want them, you do not necessarily need them. I find a woman attractive who stands on her own two feet and does not need me for anything, but is willing to make me a part of her life to help us both become better people. Most men feel the same way I do. Losers show you their true colors fairly quickly in a relationship. That's why you should always research a potential mate before you decide to engage in a relationship or sexual intercourse.

Stereotyping is not productive, so you cannot say all people who dress a certain way or act a certain way are going to be losers. It's true that many people from well-established families

Our Stupid Relationships

never live up to their surnames. What one person may deem a loser in a relationship, someone else may welcome with open arms. Why is that? Some people are happy with attention, regardless of whether a mate does not bring anything to the relationship. That problem should be addressed early in life. It is important to teach children that when they start a relationship, the mate should bring something to the table.

If you are dating a man who does not open doors for you, pump your gas, fill your tank up from time to time from his own wallet, or pay his share of the bills – run! If he would rather hang with friends than with you; neglects the children he fathered; is physically or mentally abusive; spends all his extra money on beer; doesn't have savings but buys Jordan sneakers; is not working on completing college or trade school; keeps quitting jobs; would rather sell drugs than hold a regular job; has bad credit and does not want to work on improving it; cannot articulate his goals; doesn't make you feel special on your birthday and other holidays; doesn't push you to be better, or is incapable of being a leader in his family – run!

Fellows, if a women lives with her parents with no plan for moving out because she does not want to pay bills; spends more money on her hair than she has in the bank; has student loans but hopes you will get rich and pay them off for her; is mean to your mother; chooses you over her children; allows her child to go out in public looking dirty or unkempt but looks nice herself; is in the clubs every single weekend; cannot articulate her goals; does not want to strive to get an education or a trade; does not help you with your stress when you work hard, or if she does not make you feel special – run!

My mother once told me that you train people on how to treat you. If you allow losers into your life, if you give losers the time of the day, or if you do not keep your expectations high, you will continue to find losers. If you don't allow yourself to be taken for granted, hold yourself to the same standard as you do your current or future mate, and voice your expectations, you will have a better chance of finding true love. If a person knows you refuse be treated shabbily, he or she will think twice about saying something crazy to you.

Losers want to manipulate you into doing things for them. The potential red flags are there right in front of you. A relationship should be about building something together, and not about one person doing 80 percent of the loving and working on the relationship. Losers will not do their part to make a relationship work. They will often blame you for things going wrong in the relationship. They will generally overlook their responsibilities in the relationship. They will often ask you for more than they are willing to give.

Sometimes, to find that right person, you must go through a couple of losers. Look at them as opportunities for self-improvement. Consider that they were placed in your life just to make you stronger and to help you appreciate an authentic, loving mate when he or she presents. Get losers out of your life as soon as you can. They do not mean anything for you but heartache and possibly a drained bank account. A real man

Our Stupid Relationships

opens doors for a woman, a real man will cook for a woman, and a real man will defend and protect a woman. A real woman will have her man's back, a real woman will be understanding, and a real woman would communicate openly with her mate.

Losers are everywhere, but they will only enter your life if you allow them to have an entry point. Keep your mind focused on your relationship goals and do not allow a man or woman to knock you off track. Some people are put on this Earth to derail you, and you have to realize that and keep those people out of your life.

CHAPTER SEVEN

How Can You Keep Your Mate From Cheating?

I firmly believe that if people want to cheat on their significant others, they will do so. I also believe there are some relationships that force the significant others to evaluate whether they want to seek the comfort of someone else. So many people blame themselves for their significant others' cheating on them. You cannot control another person's feelings or actions. Many people believe men do most of the cheating, but women cheat as well. From what I have seen, you can never know if your mate is cheating unless you keep your eyes peeled for clues.

You can't keep your mate from cheating if that person truly wants to cheat. People will do what they want to do, with or without a reason. The best advice is to stay focused on your relationship. Don't give your mate a reason to look for anything from anyone else. Please your mate in all facets: mentally, physically, and spiritually. Remember, there are times when you can do everything right, but your mate may still cheat. Do not blame yourself because of your mate's stupid decision.

Your mate may claim that you caused the cheating by not meeting his or her needs. That is not a valid excuse, but the frustration that can happen when one's needs are not being met is understandable. It is important to communicate with your mate that needs are not being met; this gives your mate proper respect and the opportunity to improve the situation. If your mate is unhappy or you are unhappy with your mate, communicate that and give him or her a chance to improve. If you or your mate do not want to make changes to improve the relationship, it may be time to separate. Sometimes, separating for a few days shows how much you miss one another. It is wise to separate temporarily rather than totally break off the relationship, just to see if there is hope for a future.

The cheating urge is real. So many people wonder how it would be to experience another person's touch or intimate conversation. Those urges can lead to cheating. It may be a one-night stand or it may last for years. We have all heard of situations where a baby was fathered with the "side lady." She could be a woman who is getting more attention than the "main lady," for a variety of reasons. She may offer a sense of excitement, fill a need the main lady does not fill, and she may be willing to pamper her man more than the main lady. A responsible man will speak with his mate about his needs, desires, and interests, giving the mate a chance to adjust as needed. But even if a woman does everything her mate asks of her, she may still be the victim of cheating.

Unfortunately, people cheat, and sometimes, nothing can be done about it. It is important to try to be the best mate as possible, and if the other person decides to make a stupid decision, the blame rests with him or her. Don't allow the fact that your mate has cheated make you think less of yourself. If you have put on a few pounds and your mate uses that as the excuse for cheating, you didn't need to be with that person, anyway, because he or she is not someone with whom you can spend the rest of your life. At some point in time, all people gain weight, but true love transcends weight.

People can become habitual cheaters if they believe they cannot stop themselves from cheating. Many of you know the saying, "Once a cheater, always a cheater," and that phrase may be correct, depending on why the person cheated. I maintain the hope that some people who have cheated in previous relationships can be reformed to the point they will not cheat in subsequent relationships. That's why it's important, when you are getting to know someone, to ask difficult questions, such as whether there has been cheating in previous relationships. Try to determine the situation(s) that provoked the cheating. Realize that the person many lie to you when you start the queries, but at least you've made it clear you are not afraid to ask difficult questions when it comes to your relationship. If your prospective mate has cheated in the past, you may feel you cannot move forward, but if the answer satisfies you, that can make a big difference.

It is important to remember there are people out there who do not care if your mate is in a relationship, and they will stop at nothing to get what they want. If they want your mate, they will run right over you to get him or her. You have to trust that your base relationship is strong enough to make it through the onslaught of advances he or she might receive. Even strong relationships can end with a cheating mate. A moment of weakness is all it takes for a mate to cheat. An argument can push a mate into the arms of someone else, but you should always focus on building a trusting relationship that can withstand arguments. We have all said things we regret when we are upset, so I have tried to remember not to say anything that cannot be taken back or is mean-spirited.

Don't push your mate away just because you are upset. Learn to work through the issues you and your mate have, because if there are not more cons than pros in your relationship, it can be built to a great relationship that could last forever. Love your mate and allow him or her to love you back, but be firm that cheating is not acceptable. If your mate cheats, make the decision to either forgive or end the relationship. If you decide to forgive, insist that your mate accept parameters to how he or she can rebuild trust in your relationship. Work out the problems and keep an eye out for red flags that may show he or she is cheating again.

As crazy as it sounds, many people will allow their mates to continue to cheat on them, and take them back into their arms each time. A variety of factors can cause that to happen. The person may have children with the cheating mate and does not want to break up the family. Or the person may feel the cheating mate is such a good catch that giving him or her up to someone else is unthinkable. Insecurities in yourself can also allow a mate to get away with behavior that is not normally acceptable.

CHAPTER EIGHT

The Dreaded Friend Zone

Many men have been placed in the dreaded "friend zone" by women with whom they thought they had a chance for intimacy, but then get the vibe that the relationship may not materialize into sex. The dreaded "friend zone" is a fact of life. It is a place where no man wants to remain for any period of time. Women prefer having their mates be their friends, but that is very different than being in the "friend zone," which means you are not getting sex anytime soon!

Some men can live with being in the friend zone because they are convinced they will eventually build a relationship with the woman, gain her trust, and be viewed as an important person in her life. That may be good in theory, but in reality, it doesn't happen often – although I now suspect it may happen more than I used to think it did. I have spoken with about 20 women who have said they initially had male friends whom they were not interested in sexually at first, but they eventually built sexual relationships with them. That blew my mind, because I thought about the times when I felt I was in the dreaded "friend zone," but decided to end the relationship so I wouldn't feel like I was being played. If I only would have hung in there, I may have been able to establish longer-term relationships.

My fear of looking bad to my friends caused me to end friend-zone relationships earlier than I may have needed to, but it was more important not to look like I was chasing waterfalls. As I grew older, I learned to spot friend-zone relationships more quickly and tried to keep myself from slipping into that zone. I decided I would just be a friend and not make a move to be anything else. That prevented me from feeling like I was going to be embarrassed by rejection.

Men do not like rejection, especially when they actually have feelings for the woman in question. Some men have a hard time expressing their true feelings because of that fear of rejection. Many men will not pursue a serious relationship because they're afraid their feelings will not be reciprocated. Although men are supposed to be strong, the fear of rejection will send a man running for the hills.

I remember one situation wherein I felt I was in danger of being trapped in the dreaded friend zone. I was in college, and I met a young lady who was so cute and cool. I thought I would not mind getting to know more about her. She had a fun-loving personality and she was goal-driven. Those were qualities I loved in women, and I still do. At that time, I had a fair amount of blind confidence, so I decided to give it a shot and get to know her. I turned on the charm and my comedy act, since I knew women love it when a man can make them laugh. I sparked up a conversation with her, and she turned out to be just as cool as I thought she was. We had a great conversation.

One night, we were talking, and I decided to swing for the fences. I invited her over to play strip blackjack. I was really just talking a big game; I didn't think she would really come over to my dorm room and take me up on it. When she said she was coming over, I was unprepared; I did not even have playing cards! I went around to my fraternity brothers' rooms to see if they had cards, but none of them did. I wasn't smart enough to ask the girl to come over a bit later after I had gone to the store; I was just so happy she was actually coming over. I was such a nerd that I didn't get a deck of cards, so of course, we did not play strip poker; we just sat in the room and talked. I did not achieve my goal at the time, which was to get her naked and let the chips fall where they may.

She and I still talked after that night. We continued to have interesting conversations, but they seemed to be more superficial than intimate. I did not really learn much about her as a person. About two weeks after the strip blackjack fiasco, I asked her to go out to eat with me. We went to a restaurant, and that's where I realized I was in the dreaded friends zone. We sat across from each other, and I think I made a few attempts to touch her hand or get her to sit on my side, and my advances were disregarded. I played it off as if I was just picking at her, but I decided that after the dinner, I would pull away and put my focus on someone else. We were still good friends, but that's all it was. Dang!

I frequently wondered if I missed my chance with the strip blackjack opportunity. Did I show weakness by not taking full advantage of her giving me a change to make a major move the evening she came to my room? Should I have tried to get closer to her that night, rather than just sitting across the room, taking about God-knows-what? Those were questions I posed to myself from time to time after I stopped pursuing her.

Now that I sit back and think about the situation, I realize she may not have thought I was serious, because I did not try to take our friendship to a deeper level. I was nervous because I liked her. I had put her high on a pedestal in thinking I was lucky she was even speaking to me, and that may have led to my failure in starting a relationship with her. I kicked myself for a couple of weeks, but about a month or two later, she started dating a fellow I would have not thought she would have considered for a relationship. He was a funny guy, but he was a bit immature. That may just be my jealousy or regret surfacing. She was a couple of years younger than I was, and at that time, I was more concerned with graduating and finding a job. She may have thought I would not have time to build a relationship with her. I felt better knowing she picked this other guy, which in my mind meant we probably would not have worked out anyway. Whatever the case, I wish I had gotten those dang playing cards!

The dreaded friend zone has hit many of my friends in the past. It is always funnier watching your friend be relegated to the friend zone than having it happen to you. I remember one

Our Stupid Relationships

of my friends was interested in a young lady at the college we attended. I knew he liked her, but I did not know how she felt about him. Of course, as his friend, I had to tease him about him not having a chance with her. I was fortunate to see him make his move one day.

One night after our weekly fraternity meeting had ended and we all left the room, the girl who he liked had also just gotten out of a meeting. He and I were walking the same direction to leave the building, but he stopped. I kept walking a bit but I hung back so I could snoop on him. I saw him stop to talk to her. In my mind, I was wondering when she was going to laugh at him and walk away. I really did not hope for that to happen, but we just picked at each other that way. I saw him signal her to walk with him, but she was not interested in doing that. She gave him the friendly pat on the shoulder, which meant, "Brother, you are so in the friend zone!"

I saw him start walking the other direction – away from me, with his head down – and he was obviously embarrassed, because he knew I saw him get dissed. It was so funny at the time, because he really tried to act as if he knew she would like him and that she would be honored to be with him. I guess she shut that down quickly. I talk to my friends from time to time about that night, and we still have a good laugh about it.

CHAPTER NINE

The Mythical Relationship

The "mythical relationship" is defined as one in which a person believes everything in his or her love life is going well, when the opposite is true. A naïve individual may be convinced things that are going on are not really happening. Some people believe verbal, emotional or physical abuse by a partner is just a way of showing affection or love. It is stupid to believe that, because nothing could be further from the truth. That's what makes the relationship mythical.

If you find yourself in a situation that makes you think twice about whether you should react differently, you should ask yourself if you can trust your gut. Love does not hit, manipulate, or lie. Love kisses, holds, and tells the truth. If you feel the need to ask a question of your partner, you should feel comfortable asking that question. Make sure you identify whether you have a real relationship or a mythical relationship.

The mythical relationship also refers to a situation when someone thinks he or she is in a relationship that is non-existent. Many people convince themselves they are in relationships, but they really are in relationships with themselves, because the other person may not view things through the same perspective. How many of us have heard the words, "I don't want to be in a relationship"? Some hear this statement after having a sexual encounter with a man or woman.

Sex does not constitute a relationship, although it can signify a variety of things. It can mean the other person thinks you are beautiful or handsome and therefore wants to experience sex with you. It can also mean you not going to make the person jump through hoops, and sex will not be as difficult to get from you. Sex can sometime be emotionless. Have you ever heard the phrase, "Sex is sex and just that"? A man or woman who feels that way does not have an emotional attachment to the other person. Some people are OK with those types of relationships on both sides.

If you meet someone, give the person your number and start hanging out with him or her and eventually have sex, be careful that you are not the one wanting more than the other person does. It is embarrassing and frustrating to find out you want more from the person than he or she is willing to give. If someone is emotionally unavailable but is sexually available, you have to figure out if that is what you really want. If you are OK with casual sex and you are not looking for a relationship, then that is all good. The problem comes to play when you tell yourself you are fine with just having sex but then you start to have real feelings for the other person.

Our Stupid Relationships

Getting to know someone is a process in itself. Most people are on their best behavior initially, but a true personality can surface later, and it may not be what you want to see. People tend to get into relationships with others even though they see warning signs early in the courting stage. If a person is a tad bit crazy initially, that person may be ten times worse later in life. You shouldn't ignore the warning signs when your mate is possessive, aggressive, angry, insecure, and violent. Initially those traits may only be manifest toward others, but there may come a time when that anger is turned on you. It's true that a normally calm person can also snap and do harm, but you should always keep your eyes and mind open for warning signs.

It is also important to key in on vices. If your mate is a heavy drinker, smoker, or drug user, you have to decide whether you are OK with that, and if you can handle it if it gets worse. It is difficult to complain later about these habits if you accepted them early on in the relationship. If you cannot accept them initially, it may be best not to pursue a relationship. That does not mean you cannot help your mate limit or even quit some of the vices, but in some relationships, that task ends up being a lifelong struggle that never gets better.

In reality, even a strong relationship can be nerve-wracking. Especially early in a relationship, you will wonder if your mate is truly who he or she claims to be. You'll wonder if your mate likes you as much as you like him or her, or you wonder if you should trust your heart or your mind when you start noticing little changes in your mate. It is never too early in a relationship to question red flags that you may notice. If you believe your mate is too secretive on the phone, let your mate know your expectations regarding phone usage while in your presence. Your mate may think you are being a bit neurotic or jumping to conclusions, but you have to protect yourself and do what you can to limit the possibility of looking stupid. I have been there, and I wish I had noticed the warning signs early in the relationships.

A mate will tell you everything you need to know about him or her, if you just listen and pay close attention. It takes time, but as you grow older and experience more relationships, you start to pick up on red flags, gut feelings, and intuition. You begin to see things you may have let slide in other relationships. You start understanding your worth and what you will and will not allow a mate to do to you. That is extremely important as you try to navigate the crazy world of relationships.

Being cheated on can be one of the worse things to happen to you. It deflates you, and you can have a sense of hopelessness and pain. Many times, you blame yourself for losing your relationship, and it may indeed be your fault. Did you do everything you could to support your mate? Did you do everything you could to please your mate? Did you put your mate in a situation where he or she had to leave the relationship? These are difficult questions to ask yourself. It

Our Stupid Relationships

may not have been your fault at all; you may have just picked a cheater who feels the grass is greener on the other side, because that other person does one or two things differently than you do. There have been many times when a woman decided she no longer wanted to be in a relationship with me, but later she wanted to get back involved with me. I am sure that has happened to everyone once or twice.

Trying to rekindle a previous relationship is an interesting dilemma. A friend of mine once told me she never went back to an ex, because if it did not work the first time, it was not fated for them to be together. I personally think you can go back to a previous relationship, as long as it was a healthy one to begin with. If you are thinking about going back to an abuser, alcoholic, or drug abuser, I would advise you reconsider. There is someone out there in the world who will appreciate you and choose you as a number one priority over his or her vices. Remember that your worth as a mate is based on what you believe you deserve. Some people allow themselves to be abused or cheated on because they do not have a sense of their own worth.

No one should be able to dictate your worth. You must believe you are worth the world. You deserve to be with someone whom you can build a future with, instead of someone who will make your life more complicated. If you are in love with a person who is unavailable, remind yourself you are worth the world. There is a sort of excitement that comes with the attraction to an unavailable person, but just remember that a true relationship cannot evolve from that situation. If you are **OK** with that type of treatment, go ahead and pursue it, but you may find yourself feeling stupid after the relationship – if that's what you want to call it – ultimately ends.

CHAPTER TEN

I Think I Am In A Relationship But I Am Not

Have you ever found yourself in a situation where you thought you were a relationship, but the other person didn't feel that way? I've spoken to many people, and it has become clear that a number of people have believed they were in relationships that didn't exist. They were the only person in the relationship. People usually find this out after a relationship has ended; that's when their eyes are opened to the reality. The goal should be to notice the issues while in the relationship or before a relationship even starts.

Does your mate take you out on dates? Do you go to festivals? Or do you only see your mate at midnight, even though both of you get off work at 5 p.m.? When you are in a relationship, your mate wants to speak to you frequently and see you as much as possible. You aren't given excuses for why he or she cannot see you; instead, schedules will often be rearranged so you can be together.

Don't allow yourself to be put on the back burner. It is OK if your mate is a busy person with legitimate goals to accomplish, but your mate should still set aside special time for you. Also, your mate should allow you to help with whatever is keeping him or her so busy. Ask your mate if you can help in any way. This will show you support your mate's ideas and plans, which will strengthen your relationship. If your mate does not allow you to help, don't get discouraged. It is just important that you offered to help. Sometimes it is good for your mate to know you are supportive. That's not to say you should not try to identify ways you can help. There are times your mate may not know how you can help, or he or she could be stubborn, but will need your help at some point. Just be present and supportive.

Our hearts keep us in situations that our minds know we should not be in – and our hearts win most of the time. We are human. When the heart overpowers the mind, the opportunity to make stupid decisions comes up. There is a constant battle of right and wrong in our minds and hearts. Even though we know it is wrong to respond to text that will lead to late-night cuddle sessions with people who may not be the best for us, we sometimes just can't help ourselves. Your heart wants that warm cuddle and that feeling of being loved. Your mind is sitting on your shoulders, tapping its foot saying, "You know that person ain't no good." Sometimes it even feels good to make bad decisions. You may know that the next day is going to bring arguments, loneliness, doubt, and anger with yourself. Heart 1, Mind 0.

Our Stupid Relationships

There have been so many times when I've found myself driving to meet someone, knowing I should have stayed at home. But I felt I was building a relationship, or at times, she thought she was building a relationship, but neither of us was doing that. We were just enjoying each other's company in the midst of the night. In such situations, the heart and mind were not fighting; it was more like the lust and the mind were fighting. Lust wins over the mind so many times. It wins way more than the heart, because lust does not have a stop button. The heart will at least connect to the brain more and go out for coffee. Lust wants to fly solo and have no friends.

When I was actively dating, I had to make a decision about the relationship I wanted to have. I had to ask myself if I wanted a purely sexual relationship, a friend relationship, a "kick it" partner relationship, or a relationship that contained all of the above. I found myself at different stages of relationships, depending on how I felt at the moment. Some days, I wanted to cuddle and chill. Other days, I wanted to be on the hunt, like a starving lion. And on some days, I just wanted to be with someone I could take to meet my mother and give my last name one day. Dating is a constant conflict of feelings, thoughts, emotions, and decisions. I had been hurt so much in the past that I did not want to be hurt or rejected anymore, so making decisions about starting relationships was difficult for me.

At times, I wanted to challenge myself to see if I had the guts to approach a woman. People say public speaking is the hardest thing in life to do. I disagree; walking up to a stranger and trying to spark up a conversation, knowing that the person may blow you off, is far more challenging. I remember one lady whom I really thought was cute. I had been checking her out on social media and I had seen her out in public. She was beautiful, but I did not know anything about her. I knew her brother, but I did not know her. I frequently would talk big-man talk and say to my friends and myself that if I saw her again, I was going to get her number. Yeah, right! The very next time I saw her I had the perfect opportunity to make my move, and I froze up. She was dancing right in front of me. My mind was dancing with her, but my body did not move at all. In my mind, we were doing the tootsie roll, electric slide, and moves from the movie "Dirty Dancing," and even the cupid shuffle. In all actuality, I was a wallflower, missing an opportunity.

My friends say I have a "type," but I disagree with their evaluation. They claim I prefer "girly girls," with long hair and light brown skin. They say this knowing that I have dated girls of all skin tones. The tone of the skin is not my main interest; it is the personality. There is nothing like a woman who has a great personality. A woman who is fun loving and laughs at my corny jokes, and who is independent, adventurous, and supportive, is amazing. I also prefer a woman who does not take life so seriously and can just enjoy being alive. I hated when I would meet a young lady who conformed to those criteria, and it would not work out.

Our Stupid Relationships

I truly feel men are attracted to a "catch," and women are attracted to someone who will appreciate them for who they are. How does a woman get the man she wants, and a man get the woman he wants? The key is finding someone who is in the same space as you are. This means the precise place in the timeline of relationship interests where both of you are sitting in a given moment. The timeline starts on the left, with a low interest in a relationship, and runs to the far right of the spectrum, where you are both ready for marriage. The middle is where you are ready to date.

Where are you on that timeline? Are you emotionally and physically ready to be in a serious relationship, or are you more interested in finding someone to just be cool with? Do you want "friend zone" relationships? I just shivered when I wrote that, because I know the dreaded friend zone is real. Do you want to get married one day? If you identify where you are on the relationship timeline, you can determine where you want your mate or friend to fall on that timeline.

If you allow yourself to choose someone who is not at the same place on the timeline as you are, you may allow yourself to make stupid relationship decisions. If your potential mate is close to your location on the timeline, that is great, but if your potential mate is on the far left and you are on the far right, your relationship is not going to work. The closer you are to your potential or current mate on the relationship timeline, the better off you will be. It is not a guarantee, but there's a good possibility you will be a great match.

CHAPTER ELEVEN

I Love Myself

The most important thing in life is to see yourself in a positive light. You must love yourself before you can love others. If you do not love yourself, you can never fully give yourself to another person. Think of the heart: It pumps blood throughout your body. You may not know your heart pumps blood to itself before pumping blood to any other part of the body. That means you have to take care of yourself before you can take care of others. If you do not take care of yourself, you will not have the energy to expend on others.

Some people hide their lack of confidence in themselves by either taking on a big personality and gossiping about others, or dressing in revealing clothes to get attention. These are classic signs someone may not love himself or herself enough to love in a relationship. People need to feel loved and want to feel wanted or desired. The key to happiness in a relationship is to first be happy with yourself.

Many factors may cause people to have difficulty loving themselves. First, they may not even know they are having a hard time loving themselves, because in their minds, they don't believe they have an issue. But it is hard to feel confident when a current or former mate has beaten you down mentally. If you hear something negative or do not hear a compliment every once in a while, you naturally wonder what your mate thinks of you. One of the worse feelings I ever had in a relationship was that my mate was not attracted to me or that she did not yearn for me. Those feelings can take you by surprise and really lower your self-esteem.

Love for yourself is the key to love for another person. It took me a long time to learn how to love myself. My childhood was difficult, which prevented me from learning the importance of loving myself. A bully picked on me when I was in elementary school. I also was held back in second grade, which convinced me I was not as smart as the other kids. Also, my father was not active in my life as I grew up. You may have a similar or different story about how you got to where you are right now. There may have been reasons you felt you were inadequate, unwanted, underappreciated, forgotten or unloved. Learning to love yourself can help create a healthy life. We allow ourselves to be underappreciated far too frequently. The more we learn to love ourselves, the less we will allow people who do not love us to treat us wrong.

I have found that telling myself that I love myself is very beneficial. You can tell when people have love for themselves. It is inspiring to see someone who has this type of confidence. It is not easy to do this. I struggled with self-identity while growing up, but as soon as I decided I would love myself and appreciate the person God had created, I felt better about myself. I have been a confident person most of my adult life, but I do not think I learned to love myself until later into my college days.

Whoever you are, you are a special person, and you deserve to be loved. My mother always told me you teach people how to treat you by the way you treat yourself. I think what my mother told me was a powerful statement, and it has always stuck with me. Your attitude toward yourself is outwardly manifest so others can see. For example, it is important to dress to impress. You may just need to impress yourself, but that is important. When you are dressed nicely, your hair is groomed, you smell good, and you feel good, it makes your life better. I know I feel like a different person when I have a fresh haircut and am wearing nice clothes. I also notice that people interact with me differently when I am presentable. There are more positive comments about my appearance, which feels good.

If you can dress up, you will feel up to doing anything. Your appearance reveals to others the love for yourself. It is not necessary to go out and buy a new wardrobe, but as you look at the clothes you already have, think about how they make you look and feel. If the clothes make you feel amazing, keep them. If make you feel mediocre, donate them. If you normally awaken 45 minutes before you are to be at work and you are always rushing to get dressed and out the door, change that routine. Wake up at least an hour and a half before you have to go to work so you can make yourself look the best possible. Also, you will have time to talk to yourself about how much you love yourself and how great your day is going to be. Positive affirmations are proven strategies that affectively increase the likelihood of a productive and excellent day.

Talking to yourself and praying for yourself should be a daily ritual. Your belief in a higher power is another key to loving yourself. If you feel that God loves you, it does not matter what other people think. God also wants you to love yourself because through you, his message shines. If you are having a difficult day or you are frustrated, it is important to speak to yourself about what is important. It is important that you succeed in everything you do. It is important that you control your destiny by first controlling your reactions and emotions. It is also important to be able to brush off difficulties so you can see the light on the other side of those problems. Life is designed to knock you down and challenge you. How will you deal with the challenges that come your way on a daily basis? You handle it head-on in the moment. Remind yourself that you are here on this Earth for a larger purpose: to affect change and inspire as many people as possible.

Your internal voice is extremely powerful. Do you believe your internal voice? Do you believe when you tell yourself you are loved and you are going to be successful? If you feel your internal voice is lying to you, your heart and mind are waging another battle. Your mind is trying to control you, but your heart knows how you want to feel. Continue to encourage yourself and the mind will follow. You can overcome the self-doubt that your mind pushes by continuing to speak positivity into existence. Even though I have had failed relationships, I did not give up on finding love. I knew I wanted someone who would love me unconditionally, and I did not stop or give up until I found that person. I believe my wife loves me and that she will be by my side until the end. That is real love. I could not have found her and loved her if I did not love myself.

Sometimes it is hard to love yourself when someone else has beaten you down mentally and possibly physically. If you have heard over and over that you are nothing, stupid, ugly, worthless, or unloved, it is hard to love yourself. How do you think great things about yourself when you hear so many negative things about yourself? There are so many people who stay in abusive relationships, and unfortunately, their aggressors kill some of those people.

I make sure that I let my daughter and son know I love them daily. I never want them to feel they are not loved, because I don't want them to seek that missing love from idiots. I have seen a friend verbally abuse his girlfriend; he spoke to her like she was a child. I told him he shouldn't talk to her like that and let him know she would never feel he loved her if he kept it up. He did not see anything wrong with what he was doing. I had a real problem with that. Needless to say, that relationship did not work out.

I wondered why this woman allowed him to talk to her like that. She was a few years younger than he was, so I thought that might have been the reason. But then I realized that was not a good excuse, because my girlfriend at the time was a couple of years younger than I was, and I know she would not have taken that. Most people have witnessed friends being spoken to in a disrespectful tone, and have wondered to themselves, "Why does she allow him to talk to her like that?" or "Why does he let her treat him that way?"

Words can be just as damaging as physical abuse. I never wanted to mentally abuse my girlfriend, because I enjoy being around people who are confident and love themselves. It is sexy when a lady loves herself. Also, when you are in a relationship with a woman who loves herself, she is generally happier and will be a better partner in the relationship. If you or someone you know does not has any self-love, give this friend comfort in knowing that love comes from the inside and is rewarded by a joyful life. If your friend is having a hard time with a breakup or difficult relationship, shower him or her with love and positive words. Sometimes that will not help overcome the feeling of anger, doubt, or insecurity, because some people must hear those words from a current or former mate. Those situations take time to improve. Just keep steady with your love and positive words for your friend.

You must also be prepared to have your friends be angry with you for trying to help resolve their problems. How many times has a friend or family member broken up with a mate, only to get right back together with the mate, without any improvements to the relationship? If you voice your concern with the friend's actions, you can become the bad guy or girl.

Our Stupid Relationships

Some people have to bump their heads or be burned by a fire a few times before they will wake up to the fact that they may be in stupid relationships. Be patient with your friend or family member. Be there to offer yourself as a sounding board. Choose your words about the abusive mate carefully, because those words may come back to hurt your friendship if your friend decides to stay with that mate.

I have had friends break up with girlfriends and I have said negative things about their relationships or those girlfriends. My friends have ended up getting back with the girlfriends, and it has caused a bit of a strain on our friendship, because of all the negative things I said. Some of my brilliant friends have even shared information about the negative comments I made about their girlfriends with those women, and that, of course, has caused other problems. I hate when that happens. I am sure that has happened to most people at one time or another.

Teaching love for oneself starts at a young age. It is especially critical that young ladies know they are loved, because if they do not, they may look for love from an abuser, pimp, rapist, or other type of criminal. We must hold our young ladies close and let them know they are loved and are special. We also must do our best to ensure our young ladies look presentable. They must understand how important it is to have proper hygiene and that their hair should be fixed daily, especially if they are going to be in front of other people.

I see so many young women who haven't bothered to comb their hair that day, while their mother's hair is freshly done. Our job as parents is to do everything we can to give our children a better life than our own. If your hair is done, make sure your child looks even better than you do. Even if your hair is not freshly done, ensure that your child looks presentable. This teaches our young ladies to appreciate and love themselves. Our girls will be more confident, achieve a higher education, and be even more successful because of the values instilled in them as children.

CHAPTER TWELVE

When Should I Let The Relationship Go?

We all want our relationships to work out, but in reality, not all will make it as far as marriage or last for years. Relationships are like the circle of life: They come into existence for a period of time and then die. One of the most difficult questions to ask yourself when you're in a relationship is, "When should I let the relationship go?" Many people don't want to ask themselves that, but no one should stay in a toxic relationship or one that makes a person feel stupid.

All people deserve to have someone who loves them unconditionally. Still, not all relationships are meant to end up in marriage. I believe some relationships are intended to help you grow and learn from the experience. You can learn either what you like about relationships in general, or what you hate about them. You can learn what you will tolerate and what you will not allow someone to get away with. Relationships may potentially hurt you, but you cannot allow a relationship to break you or change who you are at your core. No man or women is worth that. Our authentic "self" is all we have. We have all seen people change when they are in a relationship from whom they were when they were single. That is where relationships become unbeneficial and ultimately unsustainable.

I have many friends who believe they have to change themselves to gain the attention of the opposite sex. That even happened to me when I was younger. I felt that way in at least one past relationship; I acted differently when I was with my mate than when I was not with her. She was very religious, and I was not at that level of religiousness. I remember feeling like I had to be a bit more cautious in the way I acted around her and her family. I loved her and her family, but I never felt I could just cut loose and be myself. I now believe they would have accepted me regardless, because I was already a good kid, but for some reason, I felt nervous about how they perceived me. We sometimes allow ourselves to be influenced by what we perceive other people think of us, instead of just being ourselves. After that relationship ended, I told myself I would never allow a mate to make me act differently to the point where I felt uncomfortable.

Relationships fail because people fail. We hurt one another, we cheat, we take advantage of people, and we lie. Even though that happens as a result of our being human, it does not give anyone the right to make someone feel uncomfortable or like they have to stay in a broken relationship. Just like glass, relationships are fragile, and they can break with relative ease. A breakup can happen with even one argument, where both partners refuse to back down because they are so passionate about the points they are making. But couples should ask themselves during an argument if it is more important to win the war or the small battles. A relationship can be a set of small battles of give and take, and sometimes you have to surrender a small battle to win the overall war – which is to keep the relationship going.

If you have asked yourself when you should let a relationship go, it's probably time to do just that. Your mind will make better decisions than your heart. It is vital to use both when making decisions, but your heart will make you stay in relationships that are not healthy. Don't allow yourself to be a mental or physical punching bag for someone else. If you cannot be the first on the list, you need to remove yourself from the list.

You should think about your value when you consider how your mate is treating you. It is also essential that you are treating your mate with love and respect as well, but if your relationship seems to be a one-way street, consider breaking it off. We have heard so many stories from friends and family members who wished they had left a relationship five, seven, or even ten years before they ultimately did. So many people allow love to keep them with an unsuitable partner for years, but they are not really building anything with each other. That is unfortunate, because time is limited on this earth, and we must maximize our lives and our relationships.

It's unwise to allow your sexual relationship to hinder your everyday relationships. If your relationship has driven your friends away because they do not like the way you are being treated, look at that as a reason to evaluate your romantic partnership. On the flip side, there are some situations in which your friends will be jealous of your relationship, and they may try to sabotage it or not give it a fair chance before they pass judgment. Your friends and family generally want to look out for your best interests, and it is important to listen to their concerns, but in the end, you must decide what is best for your relationship.

Sexual relationships come and go, but personal friendships can last forever. Be mindful of your friendships and remember your friends are there for you, no matter what. Keep them close, but do not allow them to take over your relationship with your mate. Stay strong with what you believe to be true, and your truth will be visualized.

If you are in a verbally or physically abusive relationship, let that relationship go. Your life is more important than staying around to be a punching bag. There is someone out there who will offer you the world you want. Love is not abusive or manipulative, and love should not make you sad. Don't allow the hand of your mate connecting with your face to be the love you think you want. There is a saying that love doesn't cost a thing, but love does cost. It has cost lives, marriages, hospital admittances, jail time, Department of Human Services visits, and mental breakdowns.

Don't allow love to cost you the things you hold dear. And do not allow a false sense of love to make you seek security in a

Our Stupid Relationships

bad relationship. Leaving a mate is never easy, but the longer you stay in a bad relationship, the longer you will remain unhappy. You deserve to be happy, you deserve to enjoy each day on this Earth, and you deserve to feel loved. Tell yourself you will only accept a relationship that makes you happy. Once you are no longer happy, it is time to let the relationship go.

CHAPTER THIRTEEN

The Emotional Piggybank

Even the best relationships are challenging, and they require a great deal of time and effort to make them successful. There are times when you will wonder if you are being stupid in your relationship. If you have to ask yourself if you are being stupid, chances are someone else thinks you are, too. There is never a reason to hurt someone you love or who should love you. It may be difficult, but if you value yourself, you have to hold your mate to a high standard.

Relationships in general are draining, both emotionally draining and physically. So many emotions are exposed on a daily basis that it may be hard to know which one will appear in the next five minutes. Some people are more emotional than others, and they can put their mates in a whirlwind of thoughts. Not only can intimate relationships drain you, but everyday personal relationships can be taxing as well. How many times have you listened to stories from your friends or co-workers about relationships, and they just keep making the same mistakes over and over again? That can drain you.

Another situation that can take a toll on you is when you are the sounding board for all the problems of your friends,

Corey G. Carolina

family, and associates. It is important to remember you have your own problems to deal with on a daily basis, and sometimes hearing about problems from others can be overwhelming. On any given day, you may be having a great time, with things going well in your life, and a friend dumps all of his or her problems on you. I have a friend who is the sweetest person in the world. She has been there for me for over 10 years and is one of my biggest supporters. She is so emotionally available to people that I do not see how she has avoided a breakdown. I never met her mom before she passed away, but my mother told me stories of how amazing she was. I can see that trait in my friend, too.

My friend helps so many people out, creating their visions for them, and never asks for a pat on the back, compensation, or notoriety. She has been one of my closest friends for a while. I share ideas with her that no one else knows. I am confident she has my best interests in mind when I speak with her. I could not have asked for a better friend, and I want the world for her. I have seen her develop as a professional, and it is amazing to see her take charge of her life. She is an inspiration even when she may not realize it.

I know Karla Benford will continue to be an amazing friend to so many, including me. She understands the importance of an emotional piggy bank. I know she has made huge deposits into many other emotional piggy banks by withdrawing from her own. The critical step she has taken in her life is learning to set limits and saying no. The ability to say no is one of the most important traits of a successful person. I take my hat off to her, and I hope I can be as good a friend as she is. I love her more than she knows, and as I have told her in the past, I will never allow us not to be friends. That is now our not-so-inside joke.

Just as Karla does, set limits in your relationships. Do not allow yourself to be taken advantage of for any reason. Some people will occupy as much of your time for their own personal gain as they can, and they do not even realize they are doing it. It is gratifying to help others in need, but once people find out you will be available to them at any time, it can quickly burn you out. You can only help so many people with their dreams without having to put yours on hold, and that is unacceptable. Your dreams and aspirations should be the priority in your life. If your friend or mate is meant to be in your life, he or she will be understanding when you have to say "no" or "not right now." If you have your own goals and aspirations, chase after them until you accomplish them. Once you have achieved them, set new goals. Never allow yourself to be complacent.

If you feel your friend or mate is too emotionally draining for you, you may need a break. You should have no problem telling a friend or mate that you need a little break from all the stress or happenings in your life. That break may be one day, one week, or even one year. Your mental health should be your top priority in life.

If people are not depositing into your emotional piggy bank, move on. Unfortunately, some people can't help but drain your emotional piggy bank. We all know people who are the victims in every situation. The "victim mentality" is a condition from which many people suffer. There is a segment of our population that, no matter what happens, it is someone else's fault. Even though they may make bad decisions or choices, someone else is to blame. Be aware of these people. They deserve your love, attention, and affection, but don't allow them to drain your emotional piggy bank. If you feel you are a person with a victim mentality, try to change your outlook on life. Some would say you need a paradigm shift; a paradigm is a way of looking at life.

CHAPTER FOURTEEN

Sex Survival Guide

Discussing your sex life is vital to the relationship with your partner. You want to know how sexual your partner is currently feeling. Does your partner like to have sex frequently, or instead need it only on a once-a-month basis? It's important to know your partner's sex frequency preference so you will know if you can accommodate that frequency. If your partner likes to have sex four times a week but you do not want to have sex that often, this can eventually be a source of frustration. Knowing the sex frequency preference can also help you discern whether your mate could look outside the relationship to fulfill his or her frequency preference.

You also want to talk about alternatives to sexual intercourse. If there is a day when you are not in the mood for sex but your partner is in the mood, what do you do? Do you tell your mate you are not in the mood, or do you look for an alternative? If you are open with your partner, you should be able to say you are not in the mood yourself, but you are willing to find a way to give pleasure. Discuss with your partner what would please him or her if sex is not an option for you at the moment. Is the alternative oral sex, or possibly masturbation? It is important that your mate feels satisfied. He or she may just be content with your asking if an alternative sexual activity will satisfy the urge.

If your mate ever ventures outside your relationship, you want to know you tried to keep him or her satisfied sexually, and this goes both ways. Each partner must be willing to please the other for the relationship to work. If your partner is selfish when it comes to sexual activities, you should voice your concerns. If the trend continues, you should contemplate whether that person is the one you are meant to be with.

Talking during sex is a great form of communication. Your partner may not know what you like and what makes you feel good unless you explain it. When it comes to men, they often feel like they are the "kings of the jungle." Women may have to encourage them and let them know what makes them feel good. Men love noises and vocalization; it makes them feel like they are doing a great job. I do not advocate faking anything in bed, so communicating your likes and dislikes will help prevent that from happening. Women want to generally feel loved and attended to during sex. They do not want anything to be rushed; they like to savor the moment. Women also want to feel like their men are in tune with them mentally.

Have you and your partner tried "sex text"? This is a sexy form of communicating to get your partner in the mood. While you are at work, you can text your partner sweet little comments, which can quickly turn into sexual fantasies you share with your partner. You can tell your partner what you would do if he or she were in your presence. This gets your partner thinking and wishing you were there. You can tell your partner all the naughty things you want to do or that you like to have done to you.

Encouraging your partner to think about sex with you while at work will make the sex better when you get together. For example, you have Michael and his girlfriend, Samantha. They have a fairly active sex life. Michael is sitting at work, thinking about Samantha and how much he loves and misses her. He sends her a simple text message, saying, "Hi." She sends one back, saying, "Hi baby." He tells her he is feeling a little frisky and wishes she were there with him. She responds, "Well, if I were there, what would you do?" He tells her he would clear his desk and lay her on the desk. He would climb on top of her and rip her shirt off and make her scream his name. He asks her the same question, and she says she would make him scream her name while she makes him do her the way she likes to be "sexed." That text conversation will usually turn into a very good night for both parties. Try it, or something similar to it.

Withholding sex from your mate can be worse than torture for some people. I have known of people who have only had sex with their mate once or twice over the span of a year. That would not personally work for me, and it did not work for them. They were unhappy in their relationships and could not connect sexually because they felt there was no love. They did not want to have sex just for the sake of having sex. I have known other people who have sex with their mate once a month. I am floored every time I hear that. How can you claim you love someone and not show that love sexually? There may be several reasons for this deficit: You are not connected as a couple; you are not sexually attracted to your mate; you may not have the urge to be sexually active with your mate; you may be insecure with the way you look; or you may be cheating with someone else, and you have become mentally and physically unavailable to your mate.

There is an old saying that you must make love to a person's mind before you make love to the body. That's a powerful statement, because it shows that people don't just view sex as a physical act, but as a mental act as well. If you are not in tuned mentally with your mate, it will make having sex difficult. You may get the "I-just-want-to-get-it-over-with" sex, but you will not get the "I-don't-want-to-get-it-over" sex. Identifying the things that makes your mate happy will improve a sexual relationship. If your mate loves the romantic actions, do those for him or her. If your mate does not like the lovey-dovey behavior, find out what he or she does like, and do that at least every once in a while.

Sex can be an uncomfortable act. Many people are nervous during sex because there is so much going through their heads. They are wondering if their partners are enjoying themselves. They also think about specific things:

- Should I be rough or gentle?
- Should I go fast or slow?

Our Stupid Relationships

- Are those noises real or fake?

- Did she climax?

- Should I look in his or her eyes or just keep mine closed?

- Should I or should I not "go downtown"?

- What does he or she think about my body?

- How many positions should I try?

- Should I take control or allow him or her to be dominant?

- Is this just sex, or does he or she see something more with us outside of sex?

- Please let me last long enough!

- Am I better or worse than his or her last partner?

With some of these thoughts running through people's minds, it is a wonder that they can even focus on the act of sex itself. Other things can be going through the mind before, during, and after sex, and can interfere with performance. Always try to clear your mind and focus on your partner.

The key to sex in relationships is – there is no key! Sex is ever evolving. Techniques that may have turned your mate on five years ago may no longer do the job, and that is OK. You just have to communicate with your mate to see what does turn him or her on now. That young bull you fell in love with at age 24 may be a bit different at age 39. That sexy young lady you fell in love with at age 23 may not want to do some of the freaky things she did when she reaches age 37. Some people see that as a huge problem, because they feel they should continue doing the same things they did to catch their partners' interest when they first were getting to know one another. I think communication is essential in this situation, because if you stop doing something sexually without communicating with your mate, it could cause him or her to feel rejected or unloved, and it may occur to your mate that you may be cheating or seeking a way out of the relationship.

CHAPTER FIFTEEN

I Don't Mind Being Stupid

Sometimes, it may not be that bad to be stupid in a relationship. That person you fell in love with may be worth a little stupidity on your part. You may look into his or her eyes, and your heart may melt. You may tell yourself you do not mind if you look stupid in other people's eyes because you have your dream women or man you have always wanted. It is easier to feel stupid when you believe you cannot get anyone better, or if you have convinced yourself you do not want anyone else.

I know people who are well aware they are not in the best relationships they could have, but they decide to stick it out, even though others think they are stupid for doing so. That has happened to me before, too, where a friend felt I was stupid for staying in a relationship. It is hard to admit you should end a relationship. Some people feel like they have personally failed if their relationship fails. They will allow themselves to be miserable just to avoid looking stupid or feeling like a failure. Some people believe it is more important to at least get some of a mate's heart and time rather than none of it. My personal view is that relationships can affect your health, so if you allow yourself to be stressed by your mate, it could negatively impact your life.

People will stay in unhealthy relationships because they have a false sense of love from their mates. They may feel their mates love them, but in reality, the mates do nothing to show any love at all. There are times when spending time with someone, even if you know he or she is not the right person for you, may seem better than being alone. The need for companionship causes some people to make bad relationship choices. For some, there is almost nothing more depressing than sitting at home alone with no one to occupy you time. I remember when I was single, sitting at home in a dark house alone. It was boring and a bit depressing.

Humans generally have a need to be in contact with other humans. We like the conversation, the touch, the positive affirmations, and the laughs. If our need for companionship is not being met, we may allow someone with whom we generally would not waste our time to get a chunk of premium time with us. Some people are OK with being alone, and it's great if that works for them. But it does not work for me for long periods of time.

I remember my "I don't mind being stupid" moment. I met a young lady at a friend's wedding, and I instantly wanted to get to know her. She was there with a date, but I really did not care. I still followed her with my eyes as she walked to her seat. I asked the groom if the guy she was with was her boyfriend, and he said they were just friends. I swear when he

Our Stupid Relationships

said that, I felt like I had just eaten Popeye spinach and my body was all muscle.

She walked up with her date behind her to say hello to my friend. I was so happy she had come over there, because I wanted to introduce myself. The groom told her I was his friend, and she extended her hand to shake mine. I instantly wanted to hug her, but I was respectful and shook her hand. My friend was next to me, so of course, I had to act like I had some "mack game" going, though I had none. I kept shaking her hand like a weirdo. I remember telling her it was very nice to meet her and joked that she wouldn't let my hand go. She laughed, and once I got her to laugh, I just knew she would one day love me!

I saw her a couple more times during the wedding and reception, but I didn't talk to her again. A week after the wedding, I asked my friend to ask her if she thought I was cute. I realize that seems weird, and he said he was not going to ask her that. He told me he didn't want to get in the middle of the situation, because if we got together and it did not work out, it would somehow be his fault. I tried to convince him for a few days, but I was not having any luck.

A few weeks went by, and I came up with the perfect plan to meet her. The presidential inauguration of President-Elect Barack Obama was coming up, and I was interested in attending the historic event. My friend told me he had been speaking with his friend about her desire to go to the inauguration. I explained my own intentions to attend, but added that I didn't know anyone with similar plans. I convinced him to give me her number so we could discuss meeting up at the inauguration, since neither of us would know many people there. That plan worked like a charm.

He spoke with his friend and let her know I would be calling, if that were OK with her. She said she remembered me, and that would be fine. I mustered up the courage to call her, but talking about calling her and actually doing it were two different things. I was nervous! Nevertheless, I called and she picked up the phone. My throat was dry, but I knew I could not show I was nervous. We talked for about 30-45 minutes and I was mesmerized with the conversation. She was so pretty, smart, well traveled, and ambitious, and I was hooked. We discussed the presidential election and plans to go to watch the inauguration. I was unable to get a ticket, so unfortunately, I did not get to attend the historic event.

Our conversation continued daily after we initially spoke. We began to develop feelings for each other – feelings I had never experienced before. Within the first couple of months, we were talking about marriage. I remember asking her what she would say if I asked her to marry me. She replied with, "I would accept." I was shocked! We shared secrets we had not shared with anyone else, and I felt important in her life. I was so into her that I did not mind that she lived four hours away.

I had not even had sex with her, but I was drawn to her. I made a trip to see her every couple of weeks, usually staying with friends when I visited. I can't even say I thought about having sex with her very often, because I just wanted to get to know everything about her. Naturally I was very attracted to her, but I wanted to keep our relationship more mental than physical. The only other person I felt that way about was my wife, when we first started dating.

My friends told me I was getting too wrapped up too fast. But I didn't care what they said, and I didn't mind looking a little stupid for falling for someone so quickly. Unfortunately, things took a turn for the worse a few months into our relationship, when she decided to visit me for a few days. I was excited about her coming because I enjoyed anytime I could get with her. She showed up and when I saw her, my face lit up like the sun and I hugged her so tightly. I felt I would be able to see clearly where we would take our relationship after this visit.

The greeting was amazing, but that feeling did not last. The first day she was there, she annoyed me in a major way. At that time, I had a couple of dogs that were like my children, because I did not have children at the time. I remember going out to play with them for a few minutes, like I did most days. When I came back in the house, she asked, "Are you going to take a shower?" That question struck me as odd, and I asked her, "Why?" She said, "Because you have been out there with those dogs." That was the wrong comment to make. I was so upset; how dare she act like my dogs were just filthy animals? She was a girly-girl, but I had girls over before, and they would generally go outside to see my dogs. That would usually result in my male dog sniffing up their skirts or trying to jump on them. It was great!

I did not want to ruin the visit, so I kept my mouth shut and just went to take a shower. We enjoyed the rest of her first night by going out to eat and watching a movie. I slept on the couch and let her sleep in my bed. The next day was a good one until the evening. She found a place for us to enjoy poetry that evening. We got dressed and left to head to the poetry reading. The location of the event was about five minutes from my mother's house. I liked this young lady so much that I wanted her to meet my mother. While I was driving to the venue, I told her I would like to stop by my mother's house, since it is only five minutes from where we were heading. Her second mistake happened two seconds after I made that statement. She told me we would be late and that we might miss some of the poetry if we stopped.

I almost hit the roof. I thought to myself, "How did I fall for this girl? She has insulted some of the most important aspects of my life. She disrespected my dogs and now she didn't want to meet my mother!" Once again, I did not want to make a scene, so I let it go and went to the poetry reading. At that point, I was ready for her to go back home. I had totally checked out. How could someone who I started falling for treat my family so rudely? That was one thing I did not tolerate.

I played it cool for the next couple of days. I even had the chance to have sex with her, but I decided not to, because at that point, I knew I did not want to move forward with a relationship, so I did not want to complicate things further and I did not want her to feel used. I still really cared about her feelings. Over the next few weeks, I began to limit my calls, and I did not make plans to go back to see her. She became upset because I was not calling as much and I was not making routine trips to see her anymore. She wrote me a long email, apparently to voice her displeasure with my actions and me. I do not think I even responded. It was strange, because that was the fastest I had fallen for someone and then gotten over her. She is now married and happy, and I am happy for her great life. The lesson here to women is this: Never talk bad about a man's dogs, and don't diss his mother!

I felt stupid after I looked back at our relationship, because she never made an effort to have me meet her parents. I even remember her father calling when I was in her car and she asked me to not speak. I was acting stupidly, but I did not mind because I thought I was falling in love. She did take me with her to her friend's wedding, but if she loved me enough to talk marriage, why did I not get to meet any of her family? My guess is that she wanted to make sure I was who I said I was, and that I acted the same after the six-month probationary period. My feelings of being stupid and thinking I may have liked her more than she liked me were hurtful, but I got over it. I admit I did not mind being stupid for her, because even for a short time, she was very special to me. I probably ended our relationship prematurely, but I could only be stupid for so long. The red flags showed me the decision I should make.

CHAPTER SIXTEEN

Sex Does Not Make A Relationship

Sex will not keep your mate in a relationship with you, because your mate can get sex from anyone. You have to try to build a mental relationship that lets you discuss your daily thoughts with that person, who will then communicate back with you about their daily thoughts. The mental relationship lasts longer than the sexual relationship. If you plan on finding a mate to live the rest of your life with, you will at some point have a decrease in sexual appetite. If you are mentally matched with your mate, that will last forever. Sex is important, but you cannot think it is going to kick-start the relationship.

If you are into casual sex, that is a different topic altogether. Casual sex can lead to a relationship, but in my experience, it leads to even more casual hookups. Sex should not be the only thing you have in common with your mate. If you find yourself in more of a sexual relationship than an emotional or spiritual one, it is time to re-evaluate what you want from a partner and why you keep falling into these types of relationships.

Corey G. Carolina

You should never feel like you have to engage in sexual relations to keep a mate. Your virtue is more important than that. There are too many relationships wherein one person feels compelled to have sex to show love for the mate. Love does not show itself exclusively in sex. Of course, you want to have sex with the person who you love, or have strong feelings for, but sex should not be a means to making someone stick around. In fact, sex does not keep a person in a relationship. If you do not have a stronger bond, you may find your relationship does not progress beyond a sexual one.

I have known many people who have had sex with someone, only to be heartbroken because the person loses interest in a few weeks. That again goes back to being on the same relationship timeline as your potential mate. If you think someone will not show interest in you if you do not have sex, it is better to not have that person in your life rather than a source of heartbreak later. You can save yourself a lot of pain and anger if you just don't start that sexual relationship in the first place.

I have known a woman who had sex with people after knowing them for a week, and she was devastated when they stopped showing interest in her after a few months. I advised her that men are interested in the chase and capture of their prey. Just as a lion will not show interest in killing an injured gazelle because the excitement is in the chase, a man will appreciate capturing the prey only after a bit of a chase. She feels bad after she has sex with those men and is unable to build a relationship from the encounters. She is now in a relationship that started with sex with a man just one week after meeting him, but she now seems to be seeing the effects of that decision. She is now finding out her mate is not as talkative as she hoped he would be. He also is not as affectionate as she wanted him to be. Those issues can be worked out – and I hope they do work them out – but I can tell she is not completely happy. Basically, she has someone to spend her time with, and she feels the man likes her. I let her know she should continue to communicate her interests with her new mate, and actively seek from him input on his interests, to hopefully build a stronger bond.

It was also my advice that she stop having sex with men after a week of knowing them if she wants a real and lasting relationship. She is a great person, and men need to get to know her for her beautiful self. She also should allow them to get to know her mentally before they get to know her physically. She is just one of the scores of women and men who are in similar situations. My hope is that she can love and respect herself more and see the wonderful person she is, because I know one day she can make a great wife for her husband.

CHAPTER SEVENTEEN

Fly Above Your Relationship

Sometimes you have to look outside of your relationship for answers. That means it is extremely important to fly above your relationship to ensure you are not being stupid. It is extremely difficult at times to see the negative aspects of your relationship while you are in it. I missed many red flags in relationships because I was so head-over-heels in love. The red flags may not only be with your mate, but with people with whom they surround themselves and their families. That is because if you plan to build a relationship with your mate, you will at some point need to build a relationship with his or her friends and family. If you cannot build that relationship, it will be difficult to build a true relationship with your mate.

We have all known of relationships that did not work out because friends or family got in the way. Another important point is to not share everything that happens in your relationship with your family and friends. Some issues are meant to be worked out amongst two people and not seven. For example, if you decide to take a break in your relationship, your family doesn't have to know every detail as to why you took a break. That's because if you bash your mate but end up back with him or her, your family and friends may have ill feelings toward your relationship, or at least be skeptical of it, because of the previous pain or heartache your mate may have caused.

It is not easy to know how to fly above your relationship, but one way to do it is to let your mind take more control than your heart. It is also a good idea to look at your relationship as if you were counseling a friend. Pull yourself out of the day-to-day relationship and look objectively at your situation. You do not have to look only for negative traits or red flags, but it is also important to look for the positive parts of your relationship. Flying above your relationship could also help you better appreciate your mate. We sometimes get comfortable in our relationships, and we take our foot off the gas of romance. We tend to stop doing the little things that made our mates fall in love with us. We look for reasons to blame the other person for difficulties in our relationships, but if we are not giving our all and wholeheartedly working on bettering ourselves, we are a part of the problem.

Our mates deserve all of us, and we deserve all of them. We do not need to play games. We are too old for that, but some people still play games with the minds of their mates. We've all had a friend who complains about his or her mate's playing games, taking them for granted, choosing drinking over the relationship, etc., but the friend still stays in the toxic relationship. We have all asked ourselves, "Why does my friend stay in that relationship?" The answer can be simple:

Our Stupid Relationships

Some people are comfortable with the known element. That means they may allow their mates to treat them poorly, but they at least know what they have in those mates. They may be afraid of the unknown that could happen if they left their mates. Some excuses they may use are:

- I have children with my mate and I do not want to affect my children.
- If I leave my mate, I am just going to find someone else who will treat me the same way.
- My self-confidence is so bad that I can't realize what true love and compassion looks like.
- I do not want to be alone.
- Our relationship is not that bad; at least he doesn't hit me.
- He or she has cheated on me, but that's going to change.
- He or she has potential to be a provider for my family and me.
- He is just a mamma's boy.
- We have been together this long; we might as well try to make it work.
- I am unhappy but the sex is great.
- At least I get some time with him or her.

Trusting your mate can be one of the most challenging parts of a relationship, especially if you have been hurt in the past. People handle being hurt in a relationship differently.

Corey G. Carolina

Some decide they do not want to be in another relationship and just casually date. Others continue to search for love, with some of them reaching success and others jumping in and out of bad relationships. One of my goals is to help keep as many people as I can from jumping into and out of bad relationships. If you can look outside of your relationship, remove the love blinders, and see the reality of your situation, you will have more success in relationships.

Some folks are expert counselors when it comes to other people's relationships. They know just what to say to fix someone else's relationship, but when it comes to their own, they do not want to follow the same advice they have given someone else. Some people call others stupid for allowing things to go on in their relationships, but when those same things happen to them, they don't know how to handle it. You have to be able to evaluate your own relationship as if you were that expert counselor trying to give advice to a client. It's not easy to be critical of yourself or your mate but it is essential for the proper evaluation of your relationships.

The 50-foot view of your relationship could look drastically different than your street-level view. People tend to see the harsh realities of their relationship issues once they take an objective look. Looking at the pros and cons can help you identify areas of improvement that are needed in your relationship. You can perform a simple task, such as taking out a piece of paper and writing five pros and five cons about your relationship. Your pros should outweigh your cons. Even if you have five of each, the cons should hold heavier weight in your mind. Your list of pros should be positive, but if they are not, you have a problem on your hands. An example of an effective pros-and-cons list is:

PROS

1. My mate is a friend with whom I enjoy sharing my innermost thoughts.
2. I feel my mate truly loves me for me.
3. My mate wants to build a life with me.
4. I have children with my mate and she is a great mother.
5. I can't see myself with anyone else.

CONS

6. My mate doesn't seem happy in our relationship sometimes.
7. I do not feel my mate and I communicate as well as I would like when it comes to certain things that upset us about each other.
8. My mate doesn't kiss me the same.
9. My mate drinks too much and does not make me a priority.
10. My mate is not on the same level as me when it comes to trying to control debt and getting out of debt.

It is difficult to create this pros-and-cons list if you are looking at your relationship objectively. I even went through it in my own relationship, and it was eye opening, because I could not just slough off what I wanted to write down. I had to really look deeply into my marriage, and it made me think long and hard about the pros and cons, and luckily, I was able to complete my lists. Making this list will help you evaluate what truly means the most to you in a relationship. Just remember you are a strong person and nothing will break you unless you allow it to break you. Broken relationships can bring you to your knees, and you may feel your world just ended because, to a certain extent, it has.

If you adopt the philosophy that it is better to love than never to have loved at all, you will see the power in making a decision to stay in or exit a relationship. Remain strong in your faith and allow your heart and mind to work together to form the best decision. Your decision should be as close as possible to 50-50 of heart and mind input. To fly above your relationship is to take an extremely difficult step. If you are up for it, your life in relationships will be improved.

CHAPTER EIGHTEEN

Am I The Only One Working On It?

I had a conversation with a significant other one day, and I found out she had lost some attraction to me. I was devastated. I personally thought I was a handsome man and I tried to keep my appearance up and look professional. When she said that, my world came crashing down. I had never heard someone tell me that before. My former significant others may have felt that way, too, but they never told me. As a seemingly confident man, that was a blow for which I was not prepared. So many emotions and thoughts were going through my mind. The first thing I thought about was that I was not good enough for my significant other. I thought maybe I had gained too much weight or that I didn't dress well enough. After a couple of days of contemplating those things, I became angry. Who was she to tell me she had lost attraction to me? I felt if she was no longer attracted to me, then someone else would be.

I worked hard to be a good significant other. I showed her I was ambitious, driven, and a loving person, and she just stomped on my heart. I felt stupid for allowing myself to be in a situation where my significant other would think her attraction for me had decreased. The way I immediately looked at myself to see what I did wrong is the same thing that happens to thousands of others.

I truly believe that situation affected my confidence. Had other women felt the same way in the past? Did other women lose attraction to me in our relationships or casual situations? So, to put more fuel on the fire, I asked her during the same conversation, what percentage of the time that we have sex does she really want to have sex? Her answer was 50 percent. I could have hit the moon! How the hell could she tell me that? I should have been better prepared for that! I obviously asked the question because I felt she was not always into the sex we had. That is one of the worse things you can say to a man but at least she told the truth and I respected her for that.

I still think about that conversation frequently. As our conversation ended, she admitted she didn't feel great about her appearance, which is why she didn't want to have sex 50 percent of the time. Of course, to my ears, all I heard was 50 percent again. Most of you have probably been in a similar situation and can identify: You have been in a relationship with someone and fell out of attraction with him or her for some reason.

It is painful to realize you are the only one working on a relationship. Many people are in relationships only with themselves. They are not emotionally or physically connected to their mates. These couples are together for reasons other than why they initially fell in love. I do not want that type of

Our Stupid Relationships

relationship for myself, but I know that at times, difficulties will enter the relationship and I want to make sure I react in the most positive way to keep it working. I have had relationships in which I felt I was doing a majority of the communicating and trying to be truthful, but my efforts were not reciprocated. That makes the relationship dull, but when there is communication, the relationship flourishes. Sometimes I wonder what my previous relations could have been like if we had focused more on effective communication rather than just living day to day and not making a concerted effort to communicate in ways we both needed.

People do not like to fail or admit failure, but some relationships do fail. We tend to allow ourselves to stay in failing relationships because we want to force them to work. But we cannot force others to love us and to cherish us, and we cannot force them to stay in relationships with us. We have to admit failure at times and evaluate either how we can be better in our current relationships or figure out how we want to approach our next one.

The goal is to have effective and loving relationships, but it is complicated when you are the only one putting forth the effort. Your mate will generally tell you when something is wrong, either verbally or non-verbally, by his or her interaction with you. If your mate has become cold, does not answer your calls frequently, or does not do the sweet things he or she used to do, you may be working harder at your relationship than your mate wants to work.

Don't be so stubborn and refuse to see a bad relationship when it is right in front of your eyes. Don't allow someone to make you work harder in the relationship than he or she is willing to work. Remember, the relationship should be at least 50-50 in the willingness to make it work. Don't give more of yourself than your mate or potential mate is willing to give. He or she should be invested in your relationship just as much as you are. Don't be a financial supporter of your mate initially, because you may be taken advantage of. I have heard of so many relationships where two people start to get to know each other, but one person in the relationship is using the other. The user may need the mate to give him or her rides to various places because a car is out of commission and its owner is making no effort to get the car fixed. The user does not give gas money to the mate or even appreciate what this person is sacrificing to get him or her around town. Don't allow your mate or potential mate to start asking you for money early in the relationship.

I am of the old-school mindset that a man should pay for dinners initially in the relationship, but as the relationship starts to get serious, it is OK for the woman to pick up the tab every once in a while. I know men think it is attractive when a woman offers to pay for the tip. Even that small gesture shows a woman has the partnership mentality. It shows she wants to help, even though she does not have to do so. Some men would say no thank you, but they would love the offer just the same. If your mate is not giving his or her 50 percent of the

Our Stupid Relationships

relationship, communicate that you feel you are giving more to the relationship and you want to get it to the point you are both giving at least the most you can give when it comes to being physically and mentally connected.

Corey G. Carolina

Our Stupid Relationships

CHAPTER NINETEEN

Am I Stupid For Love?

Yes, you are stupid for love. Love makes you stupid at times. Love will make you do things you said you would never do. Love will make you say things you insisted you would never say. Love can consume your life. If you have the right mate, you should let love consume you. Enjoy the moments where you smell your mate's perfume or cologne and you instantly think about all the great things you experience with him or her.

It's a rare circumstance wherein a person wants to be stupid for love. People do not set out to be made to feel stupid in any situation or relationship, but unfortunately, it happens. Life is full of stupid moments, and that goes for feeling stupid in a relationship. It is not my place to tell someone he or she is stupid, because people must make decisions they feel are best for them. I can only advise it is harmful to allow yourself to be in a situation where you are being played or taken advantage of by a mate.

Corey G. Carolina

The problem with being stupid for love is that you can lose yourself in the process. Love can change you in ways you never wanted to change. I have lost friends because of decisions made in the throes of love. When I think about it, I wonder whether our friendship was worth keeping at the time. The decisions were made and the words were said, and our friendship has never been the same. Don't allow love to negatively affect you or your other relationships in your life, because you may lose someone dear to your heart.

Love may last only but for a season. You may be a person who falls heavily in love quickly. That is great, but it also makes you more open to cheating, heartache, and pain. Take a moment to understand you are vulnerable and that you fall quickly, and try something different in your next relationship. Fall in love with the process of getting to know a potential mate rather than falling in love with someone within a couple weeks. You can't get to know someone in a couple weeks. Even if you feel you have found the perfect mate, you must make sure that person is who he or she seems to be. That may take years, but remember, a relationship is a war and not just a battle. Win the war.

When you are stupid in love, you may allow yourself to be manipulated or taken advantage of because you cannot see past the love blinders. The love blinders will keep you from seeing that your mate is a gambler, heavy drinker, abusive, or a cheater. The surface of your relationship may be good, but under the first three layers, there could be turmoil.

Our Stupid Relationships

Some people can live with being stupid for love. They enjoy their mates and are willing to do anything they require. Should we look down on those people? I do not think so. If a couple wants to please each other in any form or fashion, I respect that. My personal view is people involve themselves too much in other relationships, rather than focusing on their own relationships. If all of us could mind our own business, we'd be better off.

Many people who may be viewed as being stupid in relationships have been with their mates for 15-plus years, and they are in love. Some relationships start out with cheating because one person is unfaithful to a current mate and leaves him or her to start another relationship. That new relationship has the possibility of working out even better than the previous one, but statistically, those situations are few and far between. There may be a new flavor of the month, which could cause your mate to cheat again if he or she was willing to stray on a previous mate to be with you. I do believe people can change, but my advice is to keep an extra eye out for red flags.

Plenty of folks like to criticize relationships involving couples that have been together for seven or ten years and are still not married. They become great counselors when looking at this type of relationship. It is easy to project personal judgment on someone else's relationship, but it is hard for those same people to see that their own husbands or wives are unhappy. I am not blind to that fact, either. Even as I write this book, I am thinking about my own relationship and how I can be a better mate.

Relationships are to be cherished, but some people jump in and out of them like they are insignificant. Within a relationship, you share feelings, finances, and physical property from time to time. Ending a relationship can spur cause-and-effect reactions. People must take relationships seriously to ensure they understand the ramifications of being a bad mate. Consistently being a bad mate could become chronic, and it could affect many of your relationships going forward. I am not saying you should not jump headfirst into a relationship; you should at least think long and hard before you enter into one. You should know a great deal about your mate before entering a relationship. If you were to start a business with a stranger, you would most likely ask pointed questions to ensure that partner was right for you. This philosophy is the same for choosing a new potential mate. Get to know him or her before you jump into a relationship. Get to know his or her friends and family as well. Sometimes a friend or family member will let something slip that stands as a red flag, so pay attention.

In the end, you have to protect your emotions and your body. If you try to keep yourself from being or looking stupid, you will make better decisions about your relationships. Don't let anyone play you for a fool or take advantage of you. If you are in a weakened state due to a recent breakup, keep an eye out for the wolves who can sense an opportunity to pounce.

CHAPTER TWENTY

Being Friends With An Ex

As many of us have, I have yearned for a friendship with a previous mate. I have tried to be friends with almost all the women with whom I have had a boyfriend-girlfriend relationship, so when we decided to go our separate ways, it was tough for me to lose that friendship. There are some relationships in which I regret that we ever kissed, because it affected our "friend-lationship." A friend-lationship, in my way of thinking, is a friendship that moves into a relationship. This can be the best of both worlds, because almost anyone would want to be in a relationship with another person when they know everything about each other.

Starting a relationship with a friend can be problematic. If someone knows everything about you, it can mean he or she knows when you are lying, can hold things you did in your past against you, or take advantage of you because he or she knows your weakness. It has to be a calculated risk when you decide to date a friend. I have loved all of my ex-girlfriends and even after we broke up, I had an interest in remaining friends with them. The problem is, it is difficult to be friends with someone whom you thought you might end up marrying.

Corey G. Carolina

I have had a longstanding friendship with someone who has been my best friend for years. We have seen each other go through boyfriends and girlfriends for years, but our friendship has always stayed true. We knew we would have difficult times seeing each other hurt by others, but it was important for us to always be supportive of each other. She was there for me when my heart got broken, and I was there for her when hers was broken, too. Many people thought we should have been in a relationship ourselves, but we didn't want to ruin our friendship. She has meant so much to me in my life. Many friendships are nurtured for years and are vital to another person's life. Sometimes it is better to have a best friend than a potential lover. Becoming lovers can ruin a lifelong friendship, and it is not worth the risk.

Many of my previous relationships were with women who I felt would be great partners in business and my personal life. People say I have a "type" I prefer, and that is true. My type is a woman who is driven, supportive, confident, ambitious, respectful, and genuinely nice. Looks are important, of course, as a physical attraction is imperative, but a woman with a personality is sexier than anything else. That is why it has been difficult to lose a friend when a relationship ends. If I find someone whom I genuinely enjoy spending time with and that person has the qualities I look for, not having that person around or not being in contact with her is difficult.

I know many of you have faced the same dilemma. It is so hard to find someone you want to share your life with, and when you find that person, you don't want to let go. Even though it is difficult to let someone go, it may be necessary if that person does not help you grow. If your ex does not want to be a friend, don't try to force it or try to change his or her mind. You need friends who have your best interests in mind, and not those who will take advantage of you. You should discuss a friend-lationship with your ex to see if he or she is interested in moving forward with that, or if he or she would prefer that you do not continue to build on your friendship.

Sometimes you and your ex are better off as friends than you are as mates. One difficulty in relationships is finding out where you stand with your current or former mate. You never want to feel like you are trying harder to work on a friendship or relationship than your current or former mate. I have felt stupid in the past because I finally looked at myself objectively and realized I was trying harder to make a woman want to be with me than she was working to keep me around.

There are also situations when you take a lovership to a friendship – when you decide to become friends with a previous lover. When that happens, it can be gut wrenching to see your ex-lover in a relationship with someone else. As a friend, your ex-mate may feel comfortable reverting to how you interacted before the lovership. He or she may want to share details of a new relationship, which can be tough to hear. My friend whom I spoke about earlier loved me and I loved her. I really never liked any of her boyfriends, and I do not think she really ever cared for any of my girlfriends. Deep down, I believe we wanted to be in a relationship together, but we were afraid our friendship would be affected if our relationship did not work out.

A true friend will be there for you, no matter what; a true friend will have your back when you need it, and a true friend will tell you the truth when he or she suspects you are being stupid. We hate our friends sometimes, because we know they are speaking the truth about a situation when we do not want to admit it. Allow your friends to help you become a better person in relationships. If they take your mate's side on a situation, don't disown them. It is important to have an objective friend who can provide advice. Be careful whom you seek advice from, because that person may not be the best one to give it to you. Think about how sensible your friend is, and if he or she is able to see both sides without bias. That can be tough, because your friend naturally wants to have your back and side with you. Some of my best friends have told me I was being stupid. It was hard to hear, but it was necessary for me to learn how to be a better person.

A best-friend ex, or even just a best friend of the opposite sex, can be trying for a relationship. It can be detrimental if the new mate objects to your best friend still being in your life after you were once in a relationship. If you have decided to end a relationship with your best friend and focus on a new mate, it can be hard to balance both. In one situation, you want to continue to be around and enjoy time with your best friend, but on the other hand, you want to spend time getting to know your new mate. Some people will try to bring the two relationships together and spend time together as a group, but in my experience, that does not work too well.

I remember my friend tried to have her boyfriend and me hang out with her at a bowling alley, and that turned out to be a horrible idea. First off, the dude was a jerk. Second, I just didn't like his being with her because I really wanted to be with her, but could never pull myself together enough to ask her to take our relationship to the next level. I at least tried to be a good friend and go to the bowling alley, but the whole time I was there, I was trying to find a reason to leave. I stayed because I knew my friend really wanted me to try to get to know her boyfriend.

By now, you all know you cannot force a relationship, you cannot force someone to love you, and you cannot force yourself to accept a mate who does not try to get to know your friends. Do you know your mate's friends? Have you been on a double date with your mate's friends? If your answer is no, you are not truly in a relationship. A mate who loves you or values you will want everyone who is special in his or her life to get to know you. I have a number of friends who have been in relationships with women, but one or two years has passed and their mates have never met their friends.

So how do you handle a situation where you feel your mate is purposely not introducing you to his or her friends? Communication is essential. You must voice your concern to your mate. Do not have an argument about it, but let your mate know you would like to meet his or her friends. You may even try to plan a game night and tell your mate to invite his or her friends, and you will do the same.

If that does not work or your mate makes excuses about why you have not met his or her friends or family, be patient – but not too patient. As you build on your relationship, he or she may feel more comfortable introducing you to loved ones. If you are sleeping with someone and you feel you are in a valid relationship with your mate, it is important to remember that if you are good enough to sleep with and spend time with, you should be good enough to meet his or her friends. Remember your value. If you are just having casual sex and you don't want to get too serious too soon, it may not be necessary for you to meet his or her friends. But if you are spending time together, staying at each other's houses, and in a committed relationship, you should at least know his or her best friend and have spent time with him or her.

CHAPTER TWENTY-ONE

From Lovers To Side Hugs

How many of us have seen a previous lover in public and given him or her the "side hug"? It is interesting how lovers go from being all over each other to greeting each other with handshakes, side hugs, or other unaffectionate gestures. Seeing an ex in public can be extremely awkward, because you may not know whether to say "hi" or just keep walking. The worse thing is to try to reach for a hug from your ex, who in turn reaches out with a handshake. Ouch! If you have had that happened to you or you have done this to someone, you know it sucks.

I tend to try to be cordial with my exes. That's probably because it is hard to lose love for someone with whom you once built love. If you have found it difficult to get over an ex even though you knew he or she was not right for you, you know what I mean. I hope my exes realize I want the best for them, and I hope they want the same for me. The circumstances of a breakup may determine how the public interactions will be.

During the relationship, the passion spikes, and once the relationship ends, the passion can still be there, but it can turn to strong dislike or anger. You can go from making passionate love where you are grabbing, smacking, biting, and licking to a side hug, when you see each other after the relationship is over. An ex-mate can go from saying your name in bed to not even wanting to hear your name spoken. An ex-mate can go from wanting to be tied up and spanked to walking right past an ex without speaking. I remember looking into the eyes of an ex-lover, and thinking about all the positions we have been in with each other. You can read into that anyway you would like!

The most awkward exchange I have had with an ex-lover has to be with a young lady I met at a birthday party in a hotel room. My friend and I knew her friend, so he brought me along. When I walked into the room, the birthday girl was already liquored up, and my friend introduced me to her. She immediately was into me; she gave me a tight hug and grabbed my butt. I thought that was a bit presumptuous, since I had just met her.

After we sat around and talked for a bit, I looked up and my friend had gone to the bathroom with the birthday girl's friend to have sex. The birthday girl jumped on top of me and started kissing me aggressively. I was thinking, "This is cool and weird at the same time." I was nervous because I did not know this young woman, and their friends were supposed to be coming back from the store any minute. She started grinding on me like she was ready to have sex. Even though I am a confident man, I was trying to work out in my head what was going to happen next, because I did not come prepared to have sex. It was interesting being in that situation because I felt like I was the prey and she was the tiger. I can say that was a moment when it occurred to me, "This must be how women feel!" Luckily, her friends came back into the room and my friends came out of the bathroom. They saved me from having to turn her down for sex.

I did get her number, because I liked her aggressiveness, and at that time in my life, I was not dating anyone, so I thought she might be cool to spend time with. Also, to be honest, I thought her freakiness was intriguing, and I wanted to see where our conversations and interactions would lead us. We started talking more and spending time with each other. Our relationship never materialized into a true boyfriend/girlfriend situation, but we were intimate with each other. As I assumed she would be, she was very passionate in bed. I remember one day she sucked on my bottom lip so hard that it swelled up three sizes bigger than normal. We had a great few months together, but ultimately, our relationship ended. I was not able to connect with her on many more levels than physical interest.

A few months after we stopped talking, I saw her at a grocery store. We gave each other a big hug and caught up for a few moments. We did not talk after that until the next time we saw each other, which was about eight months later – and it was a stranger interaction. I saw her at the same store. I took a step to say "hi," and she said "hi" quickly and jetted out of the store. I did not know how to take that exchange. I had heard that she had started getting more into church, so maybe I reminded her of who she was in the past. I do realize I am lucky I haven't seen her again, so I wouldn't have to figure out how I am supposed to act around her. Situations similar to this happen to many people all over the world. It is important to handle these occasions with grace and not make a scene in public or private.

I have seen all of my previous lovers in public at one point in time or another after we dated, and most of the interactions have been positive. Other than the situation with the "birthday girl," I can't remember an awkward interaction. I do remember seeing exes and suddenly wishing we were back together again. When I looked into their eyes, I saw the walks in the park. When I saw them smile, I thought of their sweet kisses and encouraging words. When I hugged them, even with a side hug, I thought about the love we had for each other and how happy I was with them at the height of our relationships.

One of my exes meant so much to me, and she will always have a piece of my heart. She was there for me when my grandfather died. That was an extremely difficult time in my life. I knew my grandfather was sick, but I did not know how sick he really was. When he started to get worse, my mother did not want me to see him in his deteriorated condition, because she wanted me to focus on my college exams. My girlfriend at the time held me as I cried, because I knew my grandfather was dying. She had unconditional love for me, and

Our Stupid Relationships

I could tell that she was in my corner. Our relationship did not work out, but she was still a special person to me at the time.

When making a decision to dissolve a relationship, you must think about the potential affects the decision may have on other people in your circle. While in a relationship, you may gain friends who were initially friends with your ex. When you break up, there is a high probability that those friends will side with their friend and not you. It can be awkward when you see friends of your ex as well. Friends of an ex can turn extremely mean once a relationship has ended.

Most of the time, how the relationship ended will determine how an ex's friends will treat you. The way you treated your ex's friends may also determine how they interact with you once the relationship is over. There are times when your ex's friends will want to keep a friendship with you, regardless of your ending the relationship with their friend. It is unfortunate that you can end up giving a previous lover a side hug after a relationship ends, but that is the nature of relationships. Some are meant to be and some are not.

Corey G. Carolina

Our Stupid Relationships

CHAPTER TWENTY-TWO

The Social Media Effect

The age of social media has changed relationships forever. You no longer get a nice handwritten note; social media has changed that to a smiley-face emoji instead. People have seen their relationships played out on the Internet for everyone to see. We have all seen those posts, some subliminal, announcing issues with a relationship. Before social media, people either called their friends on the phone to share their relationship issues or wrote them down in a journal. Unfortunately, social media has become the journal for too many people.

The reason I think social media has affected the status of relationships is because people post pictures or comments showing they broke up with their mates, but two days later, you see pictures of them back together, like nothing happened. Your relationship is meant to be private, to a certain extent. The entire world should not know everything about your relationship. If you are having problems with a spouse or mate, it is best to write those issues down or share them with a close friend. There are too many people who are on social media just to see the bad things that happen to others. They may congratulate you via social media for making a decision to post a breakup photo, but deep down, they are laughing or saying, "I told you so." Not all of our social media friends are our true friends. Some people like your page or request you as a friend just to spy on your life.

I have made it a point not to share issues with a mate on social media – mainly out of respect for my mate, but also out of respect for myself. I also do not believe in posting subliminal messages about a relationship. If you want to post something, explain the back-story a bit. We've seen too many posts that make us ask ourselves, "I wonder who or what she is talking about?" It is fine to post good news about your relationship, but the negative things should be reserved for private conversations only. If you are frequently dating, and you have a couple of relationship every two years, and you post everything that happens in your relationships it may hurt your future relationships. No one wants to date someone who is going to share all his or her feelings and problems online.

Social media is one of the most visible ways to be made to feel stupid. There are so many stories of people finding out their mates are cheating through a social media post. It's no fun to be subjected to public embarrassment on social media. Your humiliation can be viewed by thousands of people and shared with millions. It is important to have a social media

Our Stupid Relationships

conversation with your potential or current mate, because even without social media, as we know, a relationship can be very personal, passionate, emotional, and hurtful. Having the conversation with a mate to ensure both of you respect each other when it comes to social media can be critical.

The best policy is to agree not to share negative information about your relationship on social media. It is sometimes hard not to open up social media and start putting all of your feelings in a post with the relatively anonymity of a computer or phone screen, but you have to resist that urge. Even if you and your mate have this conversation, it does not guarantee an angry spouse or mate may not go back on the promise about refraining from posting negative things about your relationship on social media. You would hope you are in a relationship with an honest and trustworthy person, but anger, doubt, and loneliness are powerful emotions that make people do crazy things.

Some of the most successful relationships have been those where the mates stay off social media as much as possible. Social media has a place in our lives, and I am a lover of social media myself, but it has its function, and that is not a venue to air out my relationship issues. Plus, my wife would kill me! If we have an argument, I do not run to social media to post about it. We try to resolve it privately. I think that has helped us stay together for close to 12 years. And as it is important to keep your relationship off of social media, it is important to keep as many people as possible out of your relationship. When you tell everyone about your issues with your mate, you invite trouble. Some people scroll through social media just to look at signs of trouble in relationships.

Subliminal messages on social media are among the most annoying posts I see. There are those who will post, "I hate him!" The natural response from friends on their timeline is to ask questions. The person who posted the original message may not go into detail. Why post something like that if you do not want people to ask questions about it? That always looks like a grab for attention. I have also seen a person blast a mate online, but a week later, be posting comments about how they are back together. What message does that give people on your social media account about you? And what message does that show the mate? It indicates that you are willing to share personal information online without his or her permission. That could cause issues in the relationship, so think about that before doing it.

Social media's effect on relationship cannot be minimized, and it's the same for the Internet. There are millions of people who are cheating on their mates in their minds by chatting, viewing recorded videos, or looking at racy photos. Some folks accept this type of behavior from their mates, but others would be furious. What you will allow and tolerant is up to you. Are you OK with your mate watching porn online? Do you mind that your mate is still very good friends with his or her ex? You need to have open communication with your mate so you do know if he or she is doing any of these things. You will want to know that if you allow your mate to watch porn, will he or she be willing to do some of the with you that are being shown on these videos? There is a school of thought that porn causes people to cheat, because they want to find partners who are willing to act out some of the scenarios on the porn sites.

The Internet has brought us great things, and it allows us to instantly speak with anyone around the world. But the Internet has also become a venue for hate, gossip, and heartache. The information highway should really be used for spreading love. Social media is an Internet tool that should be dedicated to the sharing of information and positive thinking. Instead, it has become a platform for bullying, sharing secrets, and disrespecting others.

The social media effect includes all the positive aspects but also the negative aspects that come with having an online presence. Social media is brutal, and you can quickly receive backlash for something you say or a picture you post. In relationships, the less the world knows about your problems, issues, or concerns, the better. I see more negative comments and posts on Facebook than on Instagram. Facebook has become a relationship-counseling website. It is the website people use to share all their misfortunate. I am encouraged by the wonderful posts I see online, such as baby announcements, positive images, and news about promotions or entrepreneurial efforts.

Social media is like your business card to people who do not know you. It explains your political and social views, your interests, and unfortunately, your pains and issues. Social media is sometimes the first thing someone learns about you. Make the best impression by not sharing negative aspects of your relationship online. Our mates are sometimes going to upset us, but if you have to, just type the comment and delete it before you post it. You can also open a Microsoft Word document and put all your negative thoughts into one document. Save the document and keep it for viewing at a later date.

The Internet is a wonderful place to affect change, sell products, and learn about a new academic subject. Use social media for the good it was intended for, and make sure to have the conversations with your potential or current mate about your online agreement and the social media effect. That conversation can make or break your relationship.

CHAPTER TWENTY-THREE

A Person's Worth: Know Your Value

There are so many opportunities to be undervalued in relationships. Being made to feel stupid is directly related to the undervaluing of you as a person. No man or women deserves to be undervalued. But people are treated the way they allow themselves to be treated, so if you want your mate to treat you like a queen, you have to treat yourself like a queen. No one can chop down a tree when the roots are strong and fortified with grace and confidence. Your mate does not love you if he or she beats you, your mate does not love you if he or she cheats on you, and your mate does not value you if he or she talks down to you.

You are a valuable person and if your mate does not see that, it is time to move on to the next chapter in your life. No longer should you have to guess if your mate loves you, or wonder if you are giving more than your mate into the relationship, and no longer do you have to allow your mate to put you off for things they want. If you want to be in a committed relationship but the person you are dating continues to say he or she does not want that, it is time to move on to a better situation.

There is nothing more attractive than a person who is comfortable in his or her own skin and does not want to play games. A person who is genuine is hard to find, but when you find that person, your life will blossom more than you have ever thought possible. When you have the feeling that someone has got your back, it is rewarding. I am not referring to needing someone to pay all your bills or buy you nice things, but a person who will help motivate you to finish that difficult biology class, that real estate course, or start that business you have been thinking about. People are attracted to success. If you can build on small successes, you will attract successful people and people who are striving for success.

As I have repeatedly said, you are worth the world. Other people cannot dictate your value unless you allow them to, and you should never do that. Even if it feels good to hear someone tell you that you are beautiful person, or that he or she is proud of you, you should already be telling yourself the same things. Positive affirmations are important in your personal life. Living your life blaming all your problems on someone else will only keep your problems feeding off that negative energy. If you are positive even when you could be negative, you will see your personal life flourish.

A person should want to attract someone with whom he or she can help build a life. The saying, "I can do bad all by myself," is so true when deciding to bring a mate into your life. If the person you are interested in can't bring 40-50 percent more benefit to your life, you do not need him or her. I am not

Our Stupid Relationships

talking about providing good sex and companionship, because that should be a given. I am talking about helping you accomplish your short-term and long-term goals. I am talking about someone who can try to understand when you have a difficult day and not just blame it on you. I am talking about someone who will take from his or her own mental and emotional piggybank and make a deposit to yours. That is what sexy is to me.

I have seen many people who have bright futures but just do not see the value in themselves yet. We've all known people who have all the potential in the world, only to struggle to meet the expectations that are placed upon them. I think we discount the effects of how a verbally or mentally abusive relationship can affect someone for the rest of his or her life. I know a woman who started out being very energetic, passionate, and driven, but after a few bad relationships, she is no longer the same. She is no longer that driven person I knew so many years ago. She has been in a couple of relationships with men who did not value her for the great person she is. Those guys hit her, cheated on her, and mentally abused her. She now just does enough to get by. I fear that she will continue to find relationships with men who treat her like she is not a valued jewel. I look into her eyes now and I can see the years of pain, anger, and insecurities.

I want to do my part to keep as many men and women from going through things my friends and I have been through. No one deserves to be undervalued or treated like an insignificant person. Value can be real or perceived. If you want yourself to be truly valued by others, they need to see that you value yourself. I remember walking out of a hotel after attending a party about five years ago, and I was walking with my head down. A woman called out to me and said, "Young man, don't walk with your head down; keep your head up and walk with pride." I was so inspired by what she said that even now, I remind myself to keep my head up and walk with pride.

CHAPTER TWENTY-FOUR

The Unexciting Relationship

A key component to a relationship is FUN. Do you have fun with your mate? Is your relationship exciting and adventurous, or do you feel bored? It is important to spend quality time with your mate, but it is difficult if one person in the relationship is adventurous and the other one is not. My most memorable relationships were the ones in which I felt I was dating a friend who loved having fun.

Boring relationships ultimately fail. Couples must make a concerted effort to show interests in their mates' interests as a way to connect with those mates. That's a two-way street, because your mate should also want to do things you like to do, so the relationship is balanced when it comes to trying new things. My worst relationships were with women who were set in their ways and unwilling to try new things. This can go for trying out new restaurants, adventurous outdoor outings, or even sexual experiences.

I have friends who have been in bland relationships, and they have voiced their displeasure with those situations. They realize if a mate is not willing to try new things and enjoy life, it's a wasted relationship. I could not agree more. I have tried to be happy in all of my relationships and I try not to cause too much drama, but I admit I end up causing more than I should. Life is too short to live in boredom.

If your mate has expressed interest in having more fun in the relationship, traveling more, going to the movies, taking walks around the park, or any other activity, you should listen and seriously take those into consideration. Oftentimes, a mate will send you subtle messages within questions, or make suggestions that indicate wants and needs. Some questions or comments are cries for help for improvement in the relationship. If you want your relationship to work, give a little and try to do things to make your relationship exciting.

Many relationships that end had warning signs that eventually caused the relationship to dissolve. There have been a number of times when I felt bored with a relationship. I thought I cared for the woman, but the relationship was just humdrum; there was no excitement. I felt every day was the same. After a couple of relationships like that, I've learned not to allow complacency into a relationship. Of course, there will be times in any relationship when you get bored or you get annoyed with your mate because he or she does not want to do something you want to do, but when you have the opportunity to bring excitement to the relationship, do it.

Just as with the relationship timeline, there is also an excitement timeline. If your mate is interested in going out a couple weekends per month but you prefer to stay at home, there will be a disconnect. That disconnect does not have to continuously generate arguments, but it will cause some issues from time to time. If you both like to travel and you enjoy doing that together, you both may be on the same area of the excitement timeline. If you are not on the same excitement timeline, you can live with that, as long as you understand that you are going to go through some frustrating episodes. If you can get through those frustrations, you may have a great relationship, and maybe you both can work on getting closer on the excitement timeline.

There is almost nothing worse than a relationship without excitement. If you find yourself just looking at the wall or the ceiling, wondering why you are so bored, look to your left or right, and your problem might be right there. If your mate is so far away from you on the excitement timeline and is unwilling to move closer to your location on that timeline, evaluate whether you need to stay with that person. Boredom can be deadly, and even though you may love your mate, you should not be willing to waste your life being bored. Life is full of excitement, dreams, aspirations, and fulfilling relationships. Never allow someone to make you stagnant. If your mate wants to be boring, blame everyone else for problems, never think outside of the box, and just ignore your worth, it is time for a change in that relationship.

I have found myself bored in a relationship before, and I realize it was extremely dangerous. When the relationship started, I could not wait to see my mate, but as time went on, the excitement turned into annoyance. When you are irritated, even the smallest things will set you off. You do not even have to say anything, because your face will reveal what you are thinking. It is difficult to hide anger and disappointment. I found that I had to force myself to spend time with a previous mate, and that was affecting me. I cared for her, but I was bored with her. The boredom allowed thoughts of looking for someone else to intrude – someone who was more interested in having a good time and trying new things. Trying new things was the key, rather than being stuck in a day-to-day routine. Try shaking things up a bit and doing something outside of the norm in your relationship. Keep your mate on his or her toes. Don't just expect your mate to do all of the surprising or make all the arrangements for exciting activities. Take a leap and plan some exciting activities for you and your mate.

I am a people watcher, and I'll bet a good number of others are people-watchers as well. I have for years looked at the body language of people while they are in public. My mother also taught me how to distinguish a potentially good relationship from a rocky relationship, based on a person's body language in public. We were sitting in the mall food court one day and she noticed a few couples sitting and eating with each other. One couple was leaning in to speak to each other. They both were looking into each other's eyes, smiling and laughing. Another couple's interactions were a bit different. The male was leaned back, not looking his date in the eyes, and he was focused on his phone. When his date asked a question, he would not look up, and he answered in short sentences. My mother observed that the woman might be more interested in the man than he is in her. She told me that when you love someone or you are interested in someone, you look that person in the eyes when he or she speaks with you, and you smile. The third couple was even more off the chart. They weren't engaging in conversation, but

Our Stupid Relationships

were looking around, and when their eyes did lock, their eyes immediately dropped to their phones. My mother told me that couple has either just had an argument within the past day or two, their relationship is hanging on by a thread, or they have a difficult time enjoying themselves in each other's company.

Two of those three couples are examples of unexciting relationships. Another example is a bland and dull sex life. Sex is important in relationships. It does not define a relationship, but it is a key to a great relationship. I respect couples that decide to delay having sex until they know and feel comfortable with each other. I also understand that a moment of passion can erupt even with strangers who do not know each other's middle names. I advocate getting to know someone, for the most part, before engaging in sexual activities – especially if you are looking for a serious relationship.

Sex alone is not as important in a relationship as exciting sex is. I suspect most people would prefer exciting sex rather than sex that feels like an obligation. When you have great sexual chemistry, you feel more connected to your mate. When the sexual chemistry is not there, you can find yourself going months without having sex with your mate. That is painful and a bit depressing. If you are supposed to be in love with someone and you all do not show your love by pleasing each other, there is a problem with the relationship, and I suggest discussing the elephant in the room. Ask your mate why you are not having sex regularly, and hopefully, he or she will offer a legitimate explanation. You may get a list of excuses, but if do, push your mate for more clarity. Some people are not sexual beings, and it's a good idea to learn whether your mate falls into that category as early in the relationship as possible.

Just as there are relationship and excitement timelines, there is also a sex timeline. If you are on the part of the timeline where you only want to have sex once a week, but your mate is on the three to four times a week part of the timeline, there may be trouble in your relationship. Sexual frustration can turn into sexual depression. Some people feel more loved when their mates are engaging in sexual activities with them. If the mate is not engaging in the frequency of sex that conforms to the area of the timeline their mate is on, doubt and insecurities can set in on the other individual. It is natural to wonder whether a mate is cheating or has lost attraction if the sexual activities have diminished.

I have communicated with people who have been married and have had sex with their spouse twice within the year. When I was told this, I had to ask the young lady to clarify herself. She confirmed what I heard her say was what she meant. I was floored! I thought that happened only to people who were 80 years old – although I realize many people in their 80s have very active sex lives, because some of my best friends are octogenarians! I asked the young lady how could she be in a relationship with someone if she only has sex with him twice a year. She told me they had been having problems and had fallen out of love, and were no longer physically compatible.

I was sad and intrigued at the same time. I asked her where she felt things took a turn for the worse. She told me she never addressed the elephant in the room, which was the lack of

Our Stupid Relationships

intimacy. She said she always suspected he just wanted to achieve his own pleasure, and routinely would not even kiss her during sex. She said she felt like a piece of meat instead of a valued partner. Her husband suffered from what thousands of men suffer from, and that is selfishness. Many men think having pounding sex, moving like a fire is lit behind their butts, is the best way to please a woman. I remember a woman with whom I was intimate told me she does not like a man to go back and forth quickly; she preferred slow and intimate movements. That conversation threw me off, because during our first sexual experience with each other, her words kept playing through my mind. I was trying not to be selfish but I felt like I was having sex with a schoolteacher, and if I did not perform in the expected manner, I would get a bad grade. She taught me a very good lesson, and I appreciate her for the knowledge.

If your partner likes to be rough in bed but you do not, you are going to have to try to meet in the middle or compromise on some aspects of your intimacy. Maybe you should give in to being a bit wilder, if he or she does something for you that you like. You both may learn more about what you really like by trying something new and different. Don't allow your previous experiences to affect what you will or will not try in your new relationship.

Relationships are meant to challenge you in various ways. You need to be willing to set aside your previous understandings of how relationships work. You need to ask yourself what you want in a relationship, what you are willing to tolerate and what you will not allow, and how much of yourself are you going to give to a relationship. Casual relationships can be learning opportunities; serious relationships are meant to allow you to put in place all the knowledge you have collected during previous encounters. Do not punish your new mate for something a previous mate did, unless the new mate starts doing some of the same stupid things as the previous one. Love is in the air, and relationships are vital to our mental state, but never feel like you have to be in a relationship. It is OK to have standards you are not willing to compromise, but it is important to know that not everyone can meet all of your standards.

Don't let a guy who you really like get away because he is not 6 feet tall. He may have only been 5 feet 10 inches tall, but if you really like him and he treats you well, he may be the man for you. That is more important that a few extra inches of height. Don't let a woman go because she may not wear the jean size you think you prefer your mate to wear. You may lose a great woman over that nonsense. Believe me, I almost did.

LIFE'S REFLECTION

My goal in life is to leave my relationships – whether sexual, friendly, or otherwise – better than when they started. I have made a number of mistakes, and I know I will continue to make mistakes, but I have learned much from those mistakes. I know people do not deserve to be lied to, cheated on, or hurt due to my selfishness, and I hope to mend those wounds that I have caused one day.

My life has been a series of regrets and accomplishments, and I am glad that I have had people in my life willing to ride with me through both. There have been people in my life who loved me more than I knew how to love myself. There have been people in my life who have disliked me because of a failed relationship, either casual or serious, and to them I say, "I am sorry for any pain I have caused."

I am not perfect, but I have perfection as a goal. I know it cannot be attained, but the closer to perfection I can get, the better person I will become. This Earth is here for us to experience as much as possible. If you have been hurt by someone or you have hurt someone else, try to be a better person and mend that fence, even with just an apology.